Koreans

IN MINNESOTA

Sooh-Rhee Ryu

MINNESOTA
HISTORICAL
SOCIETY PRESS

mnhspress.org

The Minnesota Historical Society Press is a member of the Association of University Presses.

Manufactured in the United States of America

10 9 8 7 6 5 4 3 2 1

♾ The paper used in this publication meets the minimum requirements of the American National Standard for Information Sciences—Permanence for Printed Library Materials, ANSI Z39.48-1984.

International Standard Book Number
ISBN: 978-1-68134-133-0 (paper)
ISBN: 978-1-68134-134-7 (e-book)

Library of Congress Cataloging-in-Publication Data

Names: Ryu, Sooh-Rhee, 1979– author.
Title: Koreans in Minnesota / Sooh-Rhee Ryu.
Description: St. Paul, MN : Minnesota Historical Society Press, 2019. | Series: People of
    Minnesota | Includes bibliographical references and index.
Identifiers: LCCN 2019019604 | ISBN 9781681341330 (pbk. : alk. paper) |
    ISBN 9781681341347 (ebook)
Subjects: LCSH: Koreans—Minnesota. | Korean-Americans—Minnesota. |
    Immigrants—Minnesota.
Classification: LCC F615.K6 R98 2019 | DDC 977.6/1004957—dc23
LC record available at https://lccn.loc.gov/2019019604

This and other Minnesota Historical Society Press books are available from popular e-book vendors.

Front cover: Photo by Kevin Kamen
Back cover: Photo by Stephen Wunrow

Cover design by Running Rhino Design.
Book design and composition by Wendy Holdman.

Contents

Koreans

IN MINNESOTA

From early arrivals who laid the groundwork for a Korean community, to Korean adoptees exploring their identity and finding friendship, to Korean women immigrating with their American husbands and adjusting to a new way of life, to so many others experiencing everyday joys and struggles, Koreans in the North Star State have many stories to tell. With more than twenty thousand Koreans living in Minnesota, and close to one and a half million in the United States, Koreans are a vibrant part of America's colorful cultural mosaic.

Korean Immigration to the United States

In 2003, Korean Americans celebrated the hundredth anniversary of Korean migration, marking the 1903 arrival of the first Korean plantation workers in the Hawaiian Islands, then a US territory. Today, Koreans are the fifth-largest Asian group in the United States, comprising almost ten percent of the Asian population. As Koreans continue to settle in the "land of opportunity," many different stories have led them to cross the Pacific Ocean.[1]

The First Wave (1903–1905): Hawaii Pineapple and Sugar Plantation Workers

In the late nineteenth century, foreign powers such as the United States, Russia, and Japan put the empire of the Chosun dynasty (1392–1910) under great pressure to modernize. Then, turbulent political times and a nationwide famine brought great hardship to many ordinary Koreans. Given the opportunity to find employment in Hawaii, the first Korean immigrants mustered the courage to voyage to "America." Between 1903 and 1905, eleven different ships made sixty-four voyages to Honolulu with Koreans on board.[2]

The first wave of Korean immigration during this time consisted of 7,226 Koreans, including 637 women and 541 children. The S.S. *Gaelic* carried the first 102 Korean migrant workers (including twenty-one women and twenty-five children), who would make up for a labor shortage on Hawaii's pineapple and sugar plantations. Yankee planters had begun sugar production in Hawaii in the 1830s but struggled to recruit enough native Hawaiians to work the plantations. Since the 1850s, the Royal Hawaiian Agricultural Society had been recruiting Chinese migrant workers to fill the need for foreign labor; they began to bring in Japanese workers in 1868.

Hawaii was annexed to the United States in 1898 and was made a US territory two years later, at which point the Chinese Exclusion Act (1882) made Chinese laborers illegal in Hawaii. The plantation owners encountered a major labor shortage. While Japanese workers became the main workforce in the plantations, they also tended to strike frequently. As a result, the Hawaiian government started to actively recruit Korean workers.[3]

The Korean migration to Hawaii was largely the result of the efforts of Horace Newton Allen, an American Protestant missionary to Korea. Allen acted as an intermediary to convince the Korean king to send Koreans to Hawaii to strengthen relations with the United States. Allen published advertisements recruiting Korean workers in the *Hwangsung* newspaper. This effort to send Korean workers to the United States was facilitated by David W. Deshler, an American who was looking for business concessions in Korea and recognized the importance of Allen's political capital. As a partner of the American Trading Company in Korea, Deshler helped build local offices in major Korean ports to recruit workers nationwide.[4]

These early immigrants to Hawaii were mostly both farming and non-farming workers. A few were former soldiers, policemen, and woodcutters from cities in the northwestern province of Korea, and a small number were students who hoped to save enough from the plantation wages to continue their studies in the United States. But not all worked on the plantations. About seven thousand Koreans were scattered among different islands, and many worked in Honolulu as clerks, gardeners, cooks, and grooms and in other positions where the pay was steady.[5]

Most of them were Christians, some coming to Hawaii for religious freedom as well as for a better economic life. American Presbyterian and Methodist missionaries had begun actively converting Koreans to Christianity in 1884, and about 40 percent of the early Korean immigrants to Hawaii were already Christians. More than half of the first 102 immigrants were from the Naeri Methodist Church in the Incheon area; they were also the original founders of the First Korean Methodist Church in Honolulu. They took the lead in organizing immigrant communities around the churches that would later become the centers of Korean cultural, political, and religious activities.[6]

The work conditions on the plantations were difficult. Korean laborers worked more than ten hours a day to earn seventy-five cents—about sixteen dollars a month. Within twenty-five years, 90 percent of the Korean workers left the plantations and found work in non-farming jobs, as shopkeepers, peddlers, and restaurant workers, for example.[7]

But the influx of Korean migrant workers did not last long. After defeating Russia in the Russo-Japanese War in 1905, Japan made Korea a protectorate, shaping its government's major policy decisions. The Japanese halted Korean workers' emigration to protect their own laborers in Hawaii.[8]

In addition to the sugar plantation workers, eleven hundred Koreans were brought to Hawaii as "picture brides" between 1910 and 1924. Most of the Korean laborers were single men between the ages of twenty and thirty, creating a gender imbalance that inspired these arranged marriages, made through the exchange of photographs.[9]

These picture brides were mostly daughters of poor families in farming villages, their marriages arranged by an elder in their family. Matchmakers were also involved, many of them female relatives from the bride's home village. Other brides had their own reasons to move to Hawaii, such as to escape poverty and patriarchy. The picture bride system was supported by the plantation owners, who expected the male laborers to settle down once they had started a family.

Most Korean picture brides were Christians; some were educated in American missionary schools before coming to Hawaii. Usually Korean picture brides had group marriage ceremonies at the First Korean Methodist Church in Honolulu alongside those who had arrived on the same ship.

Having accepted their new life as wives to Korean workers in Hawaii, these women also became an important source of labor, doing field work on the plantations or providing domestic labor, such as sewing, growing and selling vegetables, and fishing and raising animals.[10]

During this time in Korea, the independence movement against Japanese occupation was at its peak, and as a result other small groups were leaving the country. About six hundred political refugees and students who were involved in the independence movement came to the United States. Among them, 541 anti-Japanese activists left Korea without passports and were accepted by the United States as "students." They studied at prestigious universities such as Harvard, Columbia, Princeton, and Boston University. During their college years, they also founded various Korean student associations that were organized throughout the nation, providing bases of support for the independence movement back in Korea. Many of those who remained in the United States after graduation settled in the Midwest and on the East Coast, establishing Korean communities in cities such as Chicago, Washington, DC, and New York and in smaller college towns. Later, as Korean communities grew to include families and nonstudents, churches rather than these student organizations became the centers of political, social, and religious activities.[11]

This wave of Korean immigration ended when the US Congress passed the 1924

A Korean mother and her baby, regular attendees at the Red Cross's monthly baby conference in Hilo, Hawaii

Immigration Act, which banned Asians from entering the United States. Korean immigration came to a standstill, and there were no notable Korean entries to the United States until the end of World War II.[12]

The Second Wave (1950–1964): The Korean War and Its Aftermath

The Korean War (1950–53) marks the beginning of the second wave (1950–64) of Korean immigration to the United States. After Korea was liberated from Japanese colonial rule in 1945, the country was thrown into the power struggle between the United States and the Soviet Union. At the end of World War II, the Korean peninsula was divided at the thirty-eighth parallel so that the United States and the USSR could oversee demilitarization and the removal of Japanese forces. South of the thirty-eighth parallel was occupied by the United States, and the north was taken over by the Soviet Union.

In 1948, each side established its own independent government with opposing ideologies. When North Korea invaded the South in 1950 to unify the peninsula under communism, the war became a proxy of larger Cold War dynamics and the division became a stalemate. An armistice was signed in 1953, but the war never officially ended. While the war caused about a million South Korean civilian casualties and about six hundred thousand in North Korea, it also led to thousands of displaced people. Many of these refugees immigrated to the United States, especially North Koreans who did not have strong family or regional ties in South Korea. Also, a small number of Korean prisoners of war were sent to the United States after refusing to be repatriated to either North or South Korea.[13]

In addition to the refugees, two groups of Korean immigrants were introduced during and after the Korean War: the so-called "war brides" and the first generation of Korean adoptees who were mainly war orphans.

Even though the US military occupation in Korea officially ended in 1948, about five hundred soldiers remained in South Korea until the outbreak of the Korean War. The war itself brought hundreds of thousands of US soldiers to Korea. Under the 1947 amendment to the War Brides Act, American servicemen could bring their Korean wives and children to the United States. Also, the McCarran-Walter Act of 1952 placed Korean wives of American servicemen in a nonquota immigrant category, removing legal barriers to entry.[14]

The presence of sizeable US forces (more than forty thousand troops) in Korea even after the war led to a continuous flow of Korean women married to American servicemen entering the United States: 292 in 1956, 1,255 in 1966, and 2,155 in 1975. By 1978, an estimated 40,366 Korean wives of American servicemen lived in the United States. These women were entitled to citizenship in just three years through their spouses and also had the oppor-

Yong Soon Lee ("Blue") (middle in photo at left) was the first Korean war bride to come to the United States. She and Sergeant Johnie Morgan met in 1949 when Lee worked for the US Army as a communications supervisor. Briefly separated by war, they soon reunited, and Lee eventually arrived in Seattle in October 1951. There, she was greeted by the press and her new American family.

tunity to sponsor their family members' immigration from Korea. In this sense, these women were major pioneers of Korean immigration to the United States.[15]

The second major group of postwar Korean immigrants were adoptees, the so-called GI babies. Often the children of Korean women and American soldiers, these Amerasian and Eurasian babies were routinely found abandoned at orphanages, police stations, city halls, and hospitals. Racially mixed children were stigmatized in Korea's racially homogeneous society, and their mothers were largely ostracized. More than 90 percent of the 2,899 children adopted out of Korea from 1953 to 1960 were of mixed parentage.

Harry and Bertha Holt, American evangelists and farmers living in South Dakota, arranged international adoptions for hundreds of American couples after they themselves adopted eight GI babies in 1955. Deeply moved by a documentary film that showed children in Korean orphanages after the war, the couple decided to do more than send money to help. While the Refugee Relief Act of 1953 limited adoption to two children per couple, the Holts were able to adopt eight through a special act of Congress (the "Holt Bill"), the result of their extensive lobbying for this exception. In 1956, the Holts established the Holt Adoption Agency (now Holt International Children's Services), which became a leader in transnational adoption. At that time, there were about five or six international adoption agencies in Korea. Each agency, including the International Social Service, would send more than a hundred racially mixed children to the United States.[16]

The practice of intercountry adoption continued throughout the 1980s, as South Korea sent orphaned and abandoned children overseas. Many of the women who gave up their children in the 1960s and '70s were primarily motivated by their poor economic backgrounds, but by the 1980s, birth mothers were more likely young and single.

Several factors, including a cultural bias against adoption and an emphasis on economic growth over social welfare policies, led to the rise of transnational adoption of babies from Korea. Between 1955 and 1977, about thirteen thousand Korean orphans and abandoned children were adopted by American families.[17]

Korean students, businessmen, and professionals also entered the United States during the second wave. Between 1945 and 1965, approximately six thousand Korean students emigrated to the United States for graduate studies, expecting that an American diploma would also earn higher social status and prestige in Korea. However, most of them did not return after completing their studies, settling instead in the United States.[18]

The Third Wave (1965–1990): The Post-1965 Korean Immigrants

Changes in US Immigration Laws

The US Immigration Act of 1965 marked the beginning of the third wave of Korean immigration. The new immigration law abolished discrimination based on race and granted equal opportunity to all countries. As a result, the largest surge in Korean immigration to the United States occurred; about fifteen thousand Korean students came between 1953 and 1980, and about thirteen thousand Korean doctors, nurses, engineers, and pharmacists immigrated between 1966 and 1979. The immigration law highlighted desirable occupational skills as a criterion to admit foreign immigrants, which explains the large percentage of Korean professionals who arrived in this wave. In 1972, 45 percent of Korean immigrants were admitted under the law's occupational immigration category.

However, as a result of the economic recession in the late 1970s and a rising unemployment rate in the United States, in 1976 Congress passed the Eilberg Act and the

Health Professions Educational Assistance Act to discourage immigration of foreign professionals. The Eilberg Act made job offers from a US employer a prerequisite for legal entry, whereas the Health Professions act required foreign physicians and surgeons to pass the exams given by the National Board of Medical Examiners to legally enter the United States. As a result, Korean occupational immigration has dropped significantly since 1979, with less than ten percent of the immigrant population being admitted under the occupational category.

By the mid-seventies, immigration based on family reunification began to shape the overall characteristics of this wave. During the 1960s and 1970s, the Korean government pursued an aggressive export-oriented economic strategy with an emphasis on the manufacturing and service industries. The decline of the agriculture sector led to a mass rural-to-urban migration, causing high population density in several large cities, especially in Seoul, where most post-1965 immigrants originated. As a result, the socioeconomic background of these immigrants tended to be lower than the earlier professional group. Still, many were urban, middle-class Koreans in white-collar professions, such as administrative, executive, and managerial occupations, before they left Korea.[19]

The higher socioeconomic status and relative success of the Koreans who arrived with professional training gained much attention, but the majority of the post-1965 immigrants were quite diverse. Despite their white-collar background, many worked in factories, engaged in clerical work, and were involved in other low-paying manual jobs.[20]

Changes in Korean Emigration Laws

While change to US immigration law was the main cause of the third wave, a Korean emigration act in 1962 had encouraged the emigration of Koreans to foreign countries.

In the 1960s, Korea was experiencing high population density, urbanization, unstable economic growth, high unemployment, and political instability. The expansion of higher education during the 1960s and 1970s led to more college graduates than the job market could accommodate. The South Korean government worked to encourage overseas immigration, expecting those workers would send home money that would increase its revenue.

The migration population under the 1962 emigration law was mostly unemployed, though educated and middle class, but it also included many North Koreans who had fled to South Korea before and after the Korean War. About seventeen thousand Koreans migrated to West Germany and the Middle East as contract mining workers, construction workers, and nurses by 1974. Some of them did not return to Korea but instead moved to the United States or Canada after their contract expired, sometimes before; the Korean government had not effectively managed the outflow of these migrant workers.[21]

As the numbers of Korean immigrants rapidly increased, the 1970s and '80s became one of the most prosperous periods for the US Korean community. Korean immigration reached its peak between 1976 and 1990. In these years, Korea was the country of origin for the third-largest group of immigrants to the United States, after Mexico and the Philippines. In addition, the Korean government twice abolished the national qualification exam that was created to discourage Korean students from going abroad to further their studies. The number of Korean students in US schools increased significantly after the government did away with the exam.[22]

Push and Pull Factors

As changes to laws and regulations in both countries encouraged Koreans to move to the United States, other factors also contributed to the mass influx of post-1965 Korean immigrants. Educational opportunities were high on the list. Extreme competition to enter colleges and high tuition at home have prompted Koreans to leave in large numbers.

The perception of the United States as the "land of opportunity" has long been a part of the American dream. Many viewed America as a second chance for those who had hopes for better economic opportunities.

The political freedom enjoyed in the United States was also a major attraction. Since the first republic was established in 1948, South Korea was ruled by a series of authoritarian and military dictators who failed to respect citizens' political rights and civil liberties. In addition to the repressive regimes of the 1970s and 1980s, South Korea's ongoing military and political tension with North Korea was another push factor explaining why so many Koreans decided to leave their home country.[23]

Recent Trends: 1990s to Present

As economic and political conditions gradually improved in Korea in the 1990s, fewer citizens chose to immigrate to the United States. A significant reduction occurred in 1991, with almost six thousand fewer Korean immigrants than the previous year. A record low was reached in 1999, with almost twenty thousand fewer immigrants than in 1990. During this time, Korea experienced steady economic growth and, in 1987, its first democratic election. These improved economic and political conditions, coupled with Seoul's hosting of the 1988 Summer Olympic Games, reversed the international image of Korea as a war-torn country and instilled a sense of national pride. Moreover, the rise of Korean global companies, such as Hyundai and Samsung, brought US–educated and –trained Korean professionals back to Korea.[24]

Koreans' perception on immigration to the United States was also altered somewhat by the 1992 Los Angeles riots.

While many Korean immigrants were well educated, urban, and middle-class, running small businesses in ethnic towns in central cities effectively isolated them from mainstream American society—not quite the status they sought. To many would-be immigrants, the LA riots further shattered the illusion of the American dream, as images of devastated Korean shop owners amid the rubble of their destroyed properties were frequently portrayed in the Korean media. Also during the late 1980s and the early 1990s, a large number of immigrants returned to Korea as the difficulties in successfully settling in the United States became a harsh reality.

However, this downward trend started to reverse in 2000. A major cause of increased emigration to the United States was the 1997 financial crisis. As the International Monetary Fund shaped major economic decisions to restructure South Korea's economy, fiscal austerity measures caused public services to deteriorate. Most of all, record levels of layoffs encouraged many to explore job options in the United States. By 2005, the number of Korean immigrants had more than doubled from its low in 1999.

From 2000 to present, the Korean immigrant population in the United States has continued to grow, with more than 80 percent of immigrants adjusting their status to become permanent residents. This percentage is significantly higher than all immigrants to the United States (59 percent), but is also higher than all Asian immigrants (56 percent). The substantial number of Korean international students, many of whom obtain professional and managerial jobs upon graduation, contributes to this high proportion. It is also increased by the presence of temporary residents, such as visiting scholars, expats, and even tourists. The fact that many Koreans have successfully adjusted their status to become permanent residents at such a high rate indicates their abilities in securing jobs with visa sponsorship. It further demonstrates their willingness to stay in the United States, implying their desire to become members of American society.[25]

Koreans in Minnesota: The First Arrivals

A Brief Overview

Who are the Koreans in Minnesota? What are the stories of their migration from Korea or elsewhere to the North Star State? What was their life like when they began to settle in Minnesota?

The size of the Korean population in Minnesota generally mirrors trends of its growth in the United States. The 1965 Immigration Act was a catalyst in the increase of Koreans in the United States as well as for Koreans in Minnesota. The highest numbers of Koreans arrived in Minnesota in 1976: 933. That year, Koreans represented 34 percent of total immigration to Minnesota. In 1990, Koreans were the second-largest Asian group in Minnesota, with a total of 11,576. They were also relatively well-off, educated suburbanites, with the largest percentage of households among Asians earning more than $50,000 a year.[26]

In 2015, there were 16,034 Koreans in Minnesota. Among them, 2,118 were US citizens born in the United States (second-generation Korean Americans), 10,197 were Koreans who became naturalized after immigration, and 2,771 were recorded as not US citizens. The remaining 948 were US citizens born abroad of American parents—most likely adult Korean adoptees. Today in Minnesota, Koreans are the fourth-largest group of Asians, making up 0.3 percent of the population. Minneapolis is home to the most Koreans in Minnesota, followed by St. Paul, Rochester, and Woodbury.[27]

The First Arrivals

Little is known about the first Korean who officially left a record of residing in Minnesota. According to the US Bureau of Labor Statistics, the Oliver Iron Mining Company reported one Korean working on the Mesabi Iron Range in 1907. The company census shows that he was over

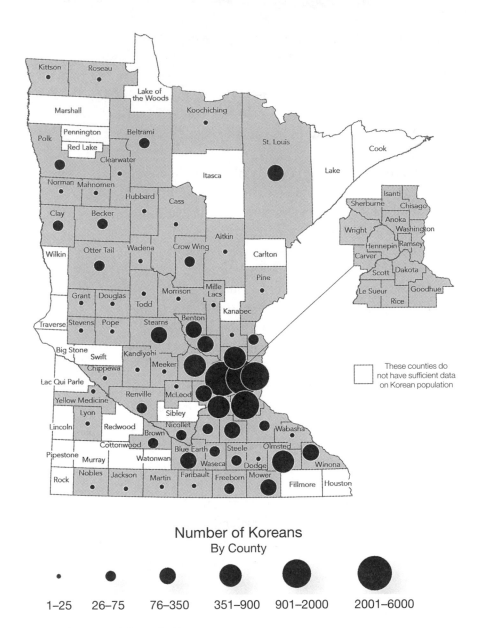

Number of Koreans
By County

•	●	●	●	●	●
1–25	26–75	76–350	351–900	901–2000	2001–6000

Minnesota Counties with Korean Residents

twenty-one years old, was married, and was not naturalized but had resided in the United States for five years.[28]

Three groups formed the early Korean population: students and faculty, wives of American servicemen, and war orphans who were adopted into Minnesota families. These Koreans migrated to Minnesota in the early 1950s and 1960s.

Korean Students and Faculty

The early Koreans in Minnesota arrived primarily as students. In the mid-1920s, two Koreans were enrolled at Hamline University in St. Paul; later, in the 1950s, more students were admitted to Macalester College, also in St. Paul. One of the first Korean students at Hamline University was Chang Suk Yun, a local leader of the Korean resistance movement against Japanese colonial rule. He was enrolled at Hamline University in 1924 and also in the University of Minnesota's summer school. He was prompted to return

The Korean Salvation Army greets new arrivals at the railroad station, 1925.

to his homeland by the tragic death by starvation of his brother and the malnutrition of his infant son.[29]

When the Korean War began, more Korean students than ever were enrolled in Macalester College, known for its cosmopolitan campus environment. Korean students were able to find social support through various programs and activities.[30]

Many of the early Korean students at Macalester were already connected to each other as family members and friends back in Korea. A small chain-migration process brought them to campus starting in the late 1940s and continued to the mid-1950s. For example, Young Pai, who arrived in 1948, was the son of Reverend Min Soo Pai, a graduate student at Princeton University. The reverend sent Young to Macalester at the suggestion of his friend Edwin Kagin. Kagin, who served as a college chaplain and chairman of the religion department at Macalester, met Young's father during his stay as a missionary in China and frequently invited Min Soo Pai to the Macalester campus.

In 1950, Young Pai invited his friend Rokwoo Shin, a twenty-four-year-old doctor who left Korea just one day before the war began, to study at Macalester. In turn, Rokwoo later brought his brother and sister, Roy Shin and Kay Shin, to Macalester, as well as a friend, Edward Chang. Philip Ahn was invited by Young Pai in 1953, then brought his younger brother Sam Ahn to Macalester in 1955. These students were actively involved in various international events and social gatherings on campus. Many of their stories and activities were regularly featured in the campus weekly newsletter.[31]

At the same time, a number of Korean graduate students and faculty at the University of Minnesota created networks as well. Some of the core people included Yun Ho Lee, a graduate student in accounting who came to Minnesota in 1953, and Yoon Bum Kim, a graduate student in microbiology. They were early members of a Korean circle

Korean student social gathering, Macalester College, 1955–56: top row left, Yun Ho Lee; middle row, left to right, Philip Ahn, Sook Lee (St. Catherine University), Soon Ja Lee, Jim Kim; front row, Sam Ahn, Edward Chang

Korean students at Macalester College: Jim Kim, Phil Ahn, Audrey [last name unknown], 1957

Philip Ahn was a member of the Korean community who came to study in Minnesota in the early 1950s. He was born in Pyongyang (today, the capital city of North Korea) in 1928. His family fled to the south in the late 1940s to escape Russian occupation. During the Korean War, his language proficiencies in English, Japanese, and Korean were highly valued; Ahn received a battlefield commission as a first lieutenant from the American military command and the Republic of Korea's army. After being discharged from the Korean Army, Philip came to Minnesota in the summer of 1953. He describes his first impression as "like a dream": "I was really surprised that most people didn't know about Korea (and the Korean War) . . . they know somebody died, twenty-seven thousand Americans died. And some people are bitter, but more people are curious."

Philip Ahn (right) at Macalester College, with Young Pai, Korean student, and C. Mazos, Greek student, 1953

At Macalester College, Ahn was known as an active international student, leading and organizing campus gatherings and events that brought international students closer together. Upon graduation in 1957, Ahn took a job in Austin, Minnesota, as a junior scientist at the Hormel Institute of the University of Minnesota Graduate School. In 1960, he became an assistant scientist at the university's medical school and worked as a physiological chemist. That year, he married Betty Engel, also a '57 graduate of Macalester.

Philip considered himself to be much more assimilated to the American way of life than other Koreans. Although interracial marriage was more common in Minnesota than in other states at that time, it was rather unusual among Koreans. While both Philip's parents and his in-laws were initially opposed to the wedding, they soon approved of the marriage and came to love the couple. Philip was proud to be a bridge between Korea and America: "Many people feel that I'm radical (because I married an American girl), but I've lived here long enough, try to bring my Korean culture into American life, and if there is an invisible wall, I have crossed. I can see both sides."

Later, he became an associate scientist in the department of food science and nutrition in the college of home economics and agriculture at the University of Minnesota. After thirty years of service as a researcher and scientist, Philip Ahn retired on June 15, 1992—proclaimed "Philip Ahn Day" by Governor Arne Carlson. Ahn continued to use his interpreting skills and experiences by assisting visiting Korean officials and dignitaries through the US State Department. He served as a board member of several local organizations, such as the International Institute of Minnesota and Planned Parenthood of Minnesota.[i]

at the university, and they took a leading role in organizing and later expanding the Korean American Association of Minnesota.

Yun Ho Lee and Dr. Joo Ho Sung, an assistant professor in neuropathology, were among just a few Koreans with jobs and families who were able to care for Korean students, many of whom were single and financially strained. Lee's home was often open on weekends for social gatherings and sharing Korean meals. Together with Sung, Lee also drove students, many of whom did not have their own transportation, back and forth to event sites in the community. Insun Hong, a graduate student in physics, was one of the early Koreans at the University of Minnesota campus but became better known as the first Korean to work at 3M.[32]

The community grew dramatically in 1955 as groups of Korean faculty members came to Minnesota. Their arrival was part of a contract between the University of Minnesota (UMN) and the Foreign Operations Administration (FOA; later renamed the International Cooperation Administration) to assist Seoul National University (SNU) in reconstructing its education and research programs that had been devastated by the Korean War. The war almost completely destroyed campus facilities and left SNU with few resources to restart many of its programs on its own. Former Minnesota governor and UMN graduate Harold E. Stassen, who was director of the US FOA at the time, arranged the project.

The exchange project involved a comprehensive and long-range interuniversity arrangement, bringing Korean administrators from SNU to the UMN to consult in the areas of agriculture, engineering, and medicine for approximately six months each. In addition, the contract also included bringing selected senior and junior faculty from SNU for one to three years to complete graduate study at the UMN. The first three engineering faculty arrived in Minnesota in 1955; in 1956, forty-four SNU faculty were

Born in 1918 in a small rural town in Korea, Yun Ho Lee dreamed of studying in the United States. While in middle school, he frequently encountered American missionaries riding their motorboats on the coastal shores of his hometown. Although it seemed far in the future, Yun Ho hoped to one day go to the missionaries' country. His dream came true when in 1949 he was admitted to study at Jamestown College (now the University of Jamestown) in North Dakota. Upon his graduation in 1953, Yun Ho pursued a master's degree in accounting at the University of Minnesota. He was employed right after graduation in 1955 by Cargill.

Yun Ho Lee doing an abacus demonstration at Cargill in 1957

Regarded as an elder and a leader, Yun Ho was the founder of the Korean American Association and the Korean Service Center, and he spearheaded the historic unification of the community's two Korean Presbyterian churches. He also successfully ran his own business, Lee's Apron Manufacturing Company. Founded in 1965, the company hired local Koreans, especially spouses of university students. The company was a major supplier for Kmart, Target, and Woolworth. Since most Korean Americans in the mid-1960s were students, businessmen like Yun Ho Lee were instrumental in providing logistical and financial support for them and other Koreans in the community.[ii]

His wife, Soon Ja Lee, included in her memoir, *My Husband, Yun Ho Lee,* recollections from several early members of the Korean community. "Unlike these days, in the 1950s, there were neither Korean restaurants nor Korean or Asian grocery stores in the Twin Cities. . . . [M]rs. Lee worked hard and long to plan and prepare authentic Korean food to entertain us and feed us the food of our homeland. . . . I also remember the fun of fellowship and the after-dinner entertainment at the Lee's home; usually a game of table tennis in his basement recreation room," recalled Dr. Johng K. Kim, who came to the University of Minnesota in 1956 as a plant genetics student.[iii]

Herb Byun, a University of Minnesota graduate and later a pacemaker design engineer at Medtronic, recalled: "I met Elder Lee first time at the Korean Christian Fellowship when I came to Minnesota as a University of Minnesota graduate student in 1975. He was already a successful businessman and a well-respected community leader. When my fiancée came to Minnesota from Korea, we could not afford to bring our parents to the wedding ceremony. Mr. and Mrs. Lee graciously took up the bride's parents' role, which we will remember forever. The Korean population in Minnesota was about 700 at that time. Whenever the word 'Korean' was in the name of an event, Elder Lee was also there, whether it was the Aquatennial Festival, Soccer Tourney, Festival of Nations, or Korean Day, he would be in the front lines."[iv]

Dr. Chong Hae Jung, who came to Minnesota in 1966 as a graduate student in art and Japanese literature, served more than forty years at the Korean church Mr. Lee attended. He especially recalled him as a very frugal person. "While Mr. Lee was known to the Koreans as a successful and wealthy businessman, he never showed his wealth in a way others would. As they say in Korea, 'in Korea clothes are the wings and in America cars are wings,' but he was not driving a Cadillac or Lincoln known to us as a symbol of wealth. We only saw him driving a big Buick."[v]

Dr. N. L. "Neal" Gault, Jr. (1920–2008) was the assistant dean of the University of Minnesota medical school when he was dispatched to Seoul in 1959 to help rebuild the medical education program at Seoul National University. He is shown here in Korea with students of SNU's rural village medical team. Dispensing support and advice, Dr. Gault dedicated much of his career to the advancement of medical education in Korea. To honor his contribution, he was named an honorary alumnus of the medical school of SNU in 1994. He also received an honorary doctorate in medicine from SNU in 2004, on the fiftieth anniversary of the UMN–SNU exchange program.

sent to the UMN. Between 1955 and 1962, 217 faculty and eight public administrators were sent to Minnesota for training and education that ranged from six months to four years. Among them, fifteen earned their doctorate degrees and seventy-one earned their master's.[33]

These UMN exchange faculty members formed a small circle of Koreans that included Minnesota's earlier arrivals. While busy studying during the week, they spent many weekends together socializing, fishing, and eating Korean food. Yun Ho and Soon Ja Lee were well known for hosting dinners at their house. "We haven't had a decent Korean meal for over five months, and when in 1957 at the end of

University of Minnesota faculty meet with Korean faculty and administrators at the Minneapolis–St. Paul Airport, April 4, 1955. Left to right: Dr. Chae Koo Lee, [unknown], Dr. Theodore Fenske, Professor Tracy Tyler, Mr. Cho, [unknown], and Yun Ho Lee.

the year about ten Seoul National University faculty including myself were invited for dinner, I couldn't forget the delicious dinner Mrs. Lee prepared, especially the taste of the kimchi she made," recalled Dr. Tae Choon Kim, who came to Minnesota as part of the exchange program in 1957.[34]

Even though the SNU–UMN contract expired in 1962 and most of the Korean faculty returned to Korea upon the completion of their studies, the influx of Korean students and faculty continued. Because of the exchange program's success, the University of Minnesota gained a high profile in Korea. Korean faculty who had studied at the UMN accomplished much, especially in the medical area. For example, Dr. Ho Wang Lee, who stayed in Minnesota from 1955 until 1959, discovered in 1976 the Hantaan River virus that had caused more than three thousand Korean and

American troops to mysteriously fall ill during the Korean War. Dr. Chang Ui Hong, who came to the UMN in 1955 in his early thirties, successfully adapted and developed the first intracardiac catheter method upon his return to Korea. And Dr. Young Kyun Lee, who studied cardiothoracic surgery at the UMN, conducted the first open-heart surgery in 1959, followed by a successful procedure in 1963.[35]

These positive outcomes inspired more Koreans to study in Minnesota. Research or teaching assistants of the already-contracted faculty were also encouraged to come to the UMN to study. A major increase in Korean enrollment occurred during the 1960s when between thirty and forty Korean graduate students attended the UMN each year. As a result, the center of Korean student life shifted from Macalester College to the University of Minnesota. Many of the students who came in the 1960s and 1970s remained in Minnesota to pursue professional opportunities. They became leaders and founding members of various organizations and institutions that still actively serve the state's Korean community.[36]

Korean Women Married to American Men

Although Korean women who were married to American men (mostly US servicemen) were among the pioneers of Korean immigration after the Korean War, their presence in the Korean community was largely invisible. Once they arrived in the United States, many settled in small towns with their American spouses and didn't encounter other Koreans. In addition to their scattered locations, their class, their educational difference, and prejudice made it difficult for these women to fully engage in the Korean community. As a result, they were more likely to assimilate to traditional American life, with very few attending Korean ethnic churches or social gatherings.[37]

JinHee Darmer, who immigrated in 1974, recalls her

early years in a small town in Wisconsin as very lonely. There were no nearby Koreans with whom she could socialize. She felt as if she were out of place; she faced discrimination at work: one colleague told her to "go back to where you come from." After moving to study at the University of Minnesota, her life started to change. She graduated with a chemical engineering degree in 2000 and worked as an engineer at 3M. She reported that "People [at 3M, St. Paul] were more open and diversified and less prejudiced against minorities." She truly felt she belonged in the workplace there.

Other challenges for this population included discrimination against their biracial children, and in many cases domestic abuse by their husbands. Even though the official public record on domestic abuse is lacking, it is widely known in the Korean community that many of these women suffered from domestic violence and that divorce was rather common. Without a formal support system, these women formed small friendship groups to help cope with hardship and provide an emotional buffer from family violence. In the early years, two attorneys in the Twin Cities, one of them married to a Korean, provided legal assistance to some of the women, but others had no such recourse. They led an isolated social life, marginalized from the Korean immigrant community.[38]

However, women who were actively contributing to the workforce were also more likely to acculturate to the American way of life. Mary Kim Bilek went through several jobs while also raising two children on her own. Upon her graduation in 1963, she worked as a supervisor of statistics for medical services at the University of Minnesota Medical School. She also worked as a senior research analyst for the Minnesota Department of Health. In 1975 she was employed by the university's College of Liberal Arts as head of data services, also becoming the college's budget and planning officer. Similarly, Kuncha Yun Johnson was a sales associate at Burnet Realty, providing Koreans with information on real estate and investment issues, while also serving as head of the Korean Women's Association.[39]

By 1980 the number of Korean women married to American men in Minnesota varied from an estimated several hundred to a thousand, but no official information was available. However, these women increased the number of Koreans in the state. JinHee Darmer praises them as pioneers of Korean immigration to the United States: "Those ladies who came here with their American husbands . . . they worked very hard and they finally settled down, and they brought their families to America." Already entitled to citizenship by marriage, they were able to sponsor family migration to the United States. Dae Hak Chi, who in the late 1970s was the owner of the Midway Oriental Foods and Gift Shop in St. Paul, was invited by his sister Nancy Brummond to take over that business in 1978. Brummond served as the first president of the Korean American Wives Association, which supported Korean women, like herself, who were married to Americans.[40]

In 1981, as more Korean women who were engaged in interracial relationships recognized the benefits of their communal gatherings, they officially launched the Korean American Wives Association (renamed the Korean American Women's Association in 2002). Today, these women are active members of Korean immigrant society, drawing people's attention to various fund-raisers, cultural events, and community activities.

Korean Adoptees in Minnesota

Adoptees' journey to find their Korean identity. Makenna Dawson shares her adoption story, which her mother calls "a miracle": "They received a picture in the mail and three months later, I arrived. Mom tells me it was the best day of her life, that hot August 4th 1995 day when she got to hold me for the first time . . . that was the day we became a family."[41]

Another adoptee, Suzanne Johnson, tried hard to find her birth parents. She appeared on a TV show that aimed to reunite adoptees with their birth families, but found no answers. "[W]ith no identifying information about my childhood, I felt lost, but with each document I received . . . I found a piece of my past. Even with these pieces, I know that the story is far from complete. . . . [I] have found solace in other Korean adoptees with whom I can share similar experiences. By learning about my birth country, its history and culture, I have been able to feel a sense of pride, replacing much of the shame I was raised to believe."[42]

Dr. Judith Eckerle, adopted when five months old, remembers a trip soon after she graduated from college: "The first time I went to Korea . . . it really changed my life and it changed the way that I thought about myself . . . it really changed my identity . . . for the first time I thought about myself as being Korean." After that visit, she went back to Korea whenever she had a chance and tried to find her birth parents. She took out an ad in a major newspaper several times and also appeared in a popular TV show that helped adoptees find their birth parents. She never found them, but she believes that passing along the love she received from her adopted family to her daughter and to other adoptees is her mission in life.[43]

"Even though I tried my hardest to fit in with white culture, and act white and be white, the fact at the end of the day was I was still Asian. I was still Korean," Chelsea Katsaros says. "That caused a lot of identity issues growing up, for sure." Katsaros was adopted when she was four months old and raised in a community that had little racial diversity. After visiting her birth country, Katsaros noticed how comforting it was to be surrounded by people who looked just like her.[44]

Kim Jackson was adopted at age four. She tried to find

her birth parents but was unable to reconnect with them. "For all the experiences that I had here [in Minnesota], it made me who I am, and I am very proud of who I am. It has taken me a long time, but I am much stronger and at peace in a lot of ways." Jackson is the art director at *Mpls.St.Paul* magazine and recently published a groundbreaking photo book called *Here* that visually documents the story of Korean adoptees in Minnesota.[45]

"I feel like I'm proud to say, I'm a Korean-American," says Susan March, who was adopted in 1975 at the age of four. While always knowing that she was adopted, March never really knew what the word *adopted* meant: "growing up in the 1970s in the suburbs [it] was hard being a minority. You don't see people that look like you and people tease you because you stand out, because you look different.... [N]ow people are more open to diversity as time passes and are able to appreciate it more." When she went to college, where there was more diversity, she became interested in Korean culture and language. There, she became active in the adult Korean adoptee community. March is glad to have found friendship, spiritual guidance through the Korean Adoptees Ministry, and, most importantly, her pride as a Korean.

Nikolas Nadeau, adopted as an infant, writes in a *Star Tribune* article that he often struggled to understand and accept his cultural identity. Only when he got into college was he forced to reconcile his Korean and American identity: "A pivotal moment came in 2006 when I enrolled in a summer Korean language program at the University of Minnesota ... [I] never felt more certain that I was, for the moment, where I belonged. After college I moved directly to Korea, where I reunited with my Korean birth mother and, for the first time in my life, experience the daily feeling of 'blending in' with my own people." While living in Korea for two years under a Fulbright Human Rights Fellowship, Nadeau worked for the Global Overseas Adoptees' Link

(G.O.A.'L.), a nongovernmental organization that provides services, such as birth family search and Korean language education, to Korean adoptees around the world.[46]

The history of Korean adoption in Minnesota. Minnesota has historically displayed an openness to domestic, international, and transracial adoption. In the nineteenth century, about five to six thousand children were sent to Minnesota via the orphan trains, nearly half of them arriving between 1882 and 1892. But more specifically, Minnesota is known as the Korean adoptee homeland. It has the highest concentration of Korean adoptees among all US states, an estimate that varies broadly between ten and twenty thousand or more since 1953.[47]

Minnesota is accommodating to adoptees for several reasons. According to Kim Park Nelson, author of *Invisible Asians: Korean American Adoptees, Asian American Experiences, and Racial Exceptionalism*, Minnesota has long been known for its progressive social politics and policies. A record of strong welfare programs, quality health care, and investment in education distinguish it as a liberal-leaning state. Minnesota's population consists mainly of descendants of Scandinavian and German Lutheran immigrants, whose cultural roots favor adoption and nonbiological kinship. Probably because of these historical factors, the state is home to numerous child welfare organizations and adoption services.[48]

Minnesota's involvement in Korean adoption began in 1955 through the Baby from Abroad program run by the Children's Home Society (CHS) of Minnesota. In 1967, CHS officially began its Korean adoption program. In 1969, Lutheran Social Service followed suit. These and other agencies such as Catholic Charities and Crossroads arranged nearly all of the eight thousand Korean adoptions occurring in Minnesota until the early 1990s.

In fact, the mid-1980s were the peak years of Korean

Kelly Sauer greets her new sister, Molly, who arrived in Minneapolis from Korea on October 8, 1981. Both girls were adopted by Patrick and Katie Sauer through Children's Home Society of Minnesota.

adoption. It is estimated that four thousand Korean adoptees resided in the state—ten percent of the total in the United States at that time. However, in the 1990s, the adoption rates for Korean children started to decline for various reasons, including that Korean families were adopting children within Korea and Korean women had better access to birth control. A higher rate of abortion also contributed to the decline. Further, the South Korean government began to prioritize domestic over international adoption, directing adoption agencies to place children within the country whenever possible. Moreover, as Korea became more recognized internationally as a significant economic player, the government was criticized for sending its children away. In 1988, when South Korea hosted the Summer Olympic Games, it was broadly and harshly described as a leader in "orphan exporting." As a result, intercountry adoption declined, and fewer Korean children were adopted in Minnesota. Lutheran Social Service brought its last Korean child to Minnesota in early 1989. In 1992, Catholic Charities brought its last Korean baby, ending a fifteen-year program, and Holt International Children's Services received its last Korean child as well.[49]

More recently, the number of newly arriving Korean adoptees has been drastically reduced to less than a thousand in 2011 and to only about three hundred in 2013. This shift is partly due to Korea's new adoption law of 2012, which tightened requirements for adoption and ensured more children were registered properly. There are also fewer Korean adoptees in Minnesota overall: 4,645 were reported in the 2000 US Census data, but only 1,265 people were identified as Korean adoptees in the 2011–16 American Community Survey.[50]

Adopted Korean children in hanbok—the traditional Korean dress—at Dual Heritage Conference, March 14, 1981

Koreans in Minnesota: 1965–Present

The Post-1965 Wave of Korean Immigrants to Minnesota

The largest group of Koreans who came directly from Korea to Minnesota after the liberal immigration law was enacted mainly consists of those who sought better economic and educational opportunities or those who connected through the family reunification program.

The settlement patterns of the post-1965 immigrants depended on several factors. Immigrants seeking to settle in the United States must apply for a visa allowing them to work legally, a process that often presents major challenges. This critical factor explains why some Koreans (and some immigrants in general) have been able to find jobs and set up new lives, whereas others have not. Between 1969 and 1972, securing permanent residency was relatively easy, but since then, it has been difficult to obtain without employer sponsorship.

Despite educated, urban, middle-class backgrounds, many post-1965 immigrants were unable to immediately gain credentials to continue as professionals in the United States. Some former professionals from Korea inevitably ended up working for hourly wages in manufacturing or became self-employed by starting their own businesses. But many who came to Minnesota to study completed school; hospital internships certified those who were in the medical profession.

As more and more Korean professionals arrived in the state, they started to form skill-based social networks. For example, Drs. Joo Ho Sung and Yoon Bum Kim organized the Minnesota Korean Medical Club in 1971. By 1980, it had thirty-five members. Aside from professional gatherings, the club also united Korean physicians who had various academic backgrounds from their years in Korea. And the club helped newly arrived Koreans who faced medical challenges because of system differences and language barriers. Other professionals formed the Minnesota chapter of a nationwide organization called Korean Scientists and Engineers; the organization participated in discipline-specific seminars and conferences back in Korea.[51]

The law schools in the Twin Cities area also provided opportunities for Koreans to pursue careers. The first known Korean law student at the University of Minnesota was Sung Chul Juhn, who graduated with a JD degree in 1980. He continued his studies at Harvard Law School and then moved to New York to be a partner in a major law firm, returning to Korea in 1991. An influx of Korean law school students began in 1992, when the UMN created a one-year master's degree designed for international students. Within twenty years, more than a hundred Koreans had completed the program and returned home to pursue their law careers.[52]

Over time, more Korean Americans came from out of state and settled in Minnesota for various reasons, such as job opportunities, to study, or to live with family. Koreans have considered Minnesota an ideal place to raise children, especially because of the network of universities and a rigorous academic environment. Also, according to Sung Won Son, "Minnesota is known to be a state of immigrants . . . much more stable in terms of population because I know most of the people, they were essentially born and raised here . . . [lending] stability and congeniality (as a congenial environment to someone coming from another country)." Son moved to Minnesota in 1974, joining the Northwestern National Bank of Minneapolis, and in 1977 became its senior vice president and chief economist.[53]

Yung Lyun Ko, founder of the Korean Institute of Minnesota, a Korean language and culture school, was a college professor back in Korea. He came to the United States in 1972 to study at Illinois State University. However, when his family arrived a year later, he decided to work to support them. Encouraged by a friend, he moved to Minnesota in

1974 to take a job at the Crown Meat Company. He was also one of the founding members of the Korean United Methodist Church that was established in 1976 in Oakdale.

Korean Americans who were brought to Minnesota in the 1970s as children recall their parents' decision to emigrate as based partly on their own educational opportunity but also as a family-oriented decision. John Choi states, "My parents were very, I think, similar to many Korean immigrants that I see. They stressed that education was really

Stephan Seung Hoe Huh, chairman/CEO at PDI Design Group, came to Minnesota for his master's degree in architecture at the University of Minnesota. "To love my country [Korea] is to succeed here in the United States," Huh reminded himself when he arrived in 1971. "My years as a student were tough but they have become beautiful memories. I came to study in Minnesota with nothing but five hundred dollars in my possession. Unlike other majors, there were no teaching assistant positions in the department of architecture, and I had to find a way to make my living. Since we [international students] were only allowed to work on campus, I started to clean the dormitory for two dollars and ten cents per hour, and later what has been known as the hardest job—cleaning the building's walls! It wasn't a lot of money, but I was amazed by the fact that I was able to buy a month['s] worth of milk and bread by working like that for a week."[vi]

Stephan Huh, chairman and CEO of PDI Design Group

First as an intern, and twenty-five years later as the CEO, Huh worked at Leonard Parker Associates. He nurtured the company through its merger with the Durrant Group in 1999 but bought it back to found PDI Design Group in 2006. Huh has been the designer, architect, and principal of numerous major projects such as the Children's Theatre, the Humphrey School of Public Affairs, the University of Minnesota Law School, the Minneapolis Convention Center, the Minnesota Judicial Center, the Minnesota Bureau of Criminal Apprehension, and many more. Today, his company is in charge of major projects all over the world, including in Korea, China, Canada, Russia, and Azerbaijan.

While making a name in the architecture world, Huh was at the same time actively involved in uniting the growing local Korean community. As the president of the Korean American Association of Minnesota, he played a critical role in Governor Rudy Perpich's proclamation of Korean Day in Minnesota in 1977. He was also one of the founding members of the Korean Institute of Minnesota, the Korean Chamber of Commerce, and the Minnesota Asian American Chamber of Commerce.

important. Doing well in school was probably the most important priority that my parents had for myself and for my sister. I see that as very typical amongst many Korean immigrants and, sometimes, maybe even too much the way they're stressing the school, putting the pressure on to do well in school." Choi's father came to the University of Minnesota for his graduate study. He did not finish his degree, but instead worked multiple jobs, including at Coca-Cola and as a reporter for the *Korean Central Daily Newspaper* (*Joongang Ilbo*).

Jong Bum Kwon shared a similar story of his parents' immigration experience in a 1994 interview with the Minnesota Historical Society. Kwon's family was invited to live

Though serving as the forty-ninth president of the Korean American Association of Minnesota, Hyun Sook Han is better known as a pioneer in the area of Korean adoption. Han was born in 1938 as the oldest of ten children. Three of the youngest children died; illness and starvation were common during the escape from North Korean forces at the onset of the Korean War. As a witness to war's devastation, Han was heartbroken: "I saw so many babies and children were crying in the snow, abandoned or lost. And I just couldn't watch them because of [feeling] guilty. I was too young to help all those children." She was only in fifth grade, but she was determined to pursue a career that would empower her to help. She chose social work.

Upon her graduation from Ewha Womans University, Hyun Sook accepted a job with International Social Service, which was coordinating American adoptions of racially mixed children born in Korea since the American occupation. In 1971 she was selected by the Council of International Programs to study and train at the University of Minnesota School of Social Work and the Children's Home Society (CHS). In 1975, she moved to Minnesota when she was contracted by CHS to work as an international adoption social worker. In this role, she expanded Korean adoptions and developed support services in Minnesota.

In her memoir, *Many Lives Intertwined*, she shares her first encounter with her American neighbors and how surprised she was to find many adoptive parents in her neighborhood:

When we were looking at houses in Highland Park [in St. Paul], I remember some of the neighborhood people watching us carefully. . . . We were the first Korean family to move into the area, and I often wondered if people thought their property values would decline because of the "Orientals." But we soon found out how much we all had in common. Shortly after we moved in, one of the neighbor ladies came by to introduce herself. We talked a while and she asked me if my husband was a medical doctor. I told her no, he was not. Does he teach at the University of Minnesota, she asked? No, he just works at a company. She was surprised, and even more so when she found out that I worked full-time as a social worker. However, she was not the [only] one to remain taken aback; my surprise in Beloit, Wisconsin, in 1976 by his mother's sister, who was married to an American serviceman. Kwon's parents came to the United States for a better life for their family but had to go through many hardships to provide for their children and support their children's education. His father was a paralegal in Korea but worked at a factory that made gearboxes for irrigation systems: "When my father was working in Korea . . . he'd wear suits every day. When he got to the United States, working in a factory, he started out at the absolute bottom. . . . [He] swept floors, mopped floors, cleaned toilets. For a thirty-three-year-old man to do that, it was very difficult on my father." His mother worked night shifts as a nurse's assistant at Carlyle Nursing Homes. In

was the discovery that she was an adoptive parent who had adopted a son and a daughter from the agency I worked for. Soon, word got out around the neighborhood that I was a social worker at [CHS], and I found out that several families in the area were adoptive families themselves, either from [CHS] or Catholic Charities or Lutheran Social Services.[vii]

Hyun Sook Han

She recalls her immigration experience as better than most. She already had a job, and her husband had previous experience with other countries and also with Americans. They both spoke English, and her husband faced few challenges applying for jobs in Minnesota. "But emotional adjustment and family life toughness is the same like other [immigrant] families. Because of the pressure and fear . . . all those emotional feelings [complicated] family life."

Governors Rudy Perpich in 1989 and Tim Pawlenty in 2004 each formally honored her with Han Hyun Sook Day for her service and contributions to the state of Minnesota. In the Korean community she was also well known as the person who spearheaded the search for a bone marrow transplant match for Brian Sung Duk Bauman, a Korean adoptee who was diagnosed with chronic myelogenous leukemia in 1995.[viii]

John J. Choi has been the Ramsey County attorney general since 2011. He is the first Asian American county attorney in Minnesota, and also the first Korean American to hold the position of chief prosecutor in the United States. Choi came to Minnesota with his parents in 1973 at the age of three: "My parents were looking for a better life. . . . They never thought their son would be elected county attorney." Raised by a typical Korean immigrant family, Choi recalls his childhood and his parents' efforts as "a story really about hard work." Choi grew up in what he calls the working-class part of Eagan that was at that time predominantly white; his family was the "lone Asian family" in the neighborhood. "Back then, in the 1970s and 1980s, no one really talked about [other cultures and races], or it wasn't something that was encouraged . . . [people] didn't really have exposure to other cultures." Choi believes our society has come a long way in terms of accepting other cultures: "[T]he fact that someone like me could become elected as Ramsey County attorney, that's what makes people feel so good about this country. I think that's the beauty of this country and why my particular election was very captivating for people who have been here for many, many years."

Before becoming a county attorney, Choi spent a decade in private practice; then he decided to devote his career to the public sector. He ran his first campaign in 2010 on issues such as battling gang violence, stopping domestic abuse, and preventing juvenile crime. In 2018, Choi was reelected for his third term.

John Choi (second from right) in 2011 with his father and members of the Korean American Association of Minnesota

1986, after ten years of tireless labor and constant saving, his parents were able to buy and operate a Laundromat.

Similarly, Sarah Imm, who came to the United States in 1974 at the age of two and a half, remembers her parents studying, working, and facing language difficulties. While her father was studying at the University of Minnesota architecture program, her mother was working to support the family. She said, "[My parents] saw this thing in *Time Magazine*. This is Minnesota Governor Wendell Anderson. And it says, 'The Good Life in Minnesota.' And he's holding a fish. And this is about Minnesota. And they saw this in a magazine and they thought, wow, this sounds like a great place."

The Mid-1970s and the 1980s: The Arrival of Blue-Collar Workers

An interesting feature of Minnesota's Korean business community is that it hasn't formed an ethnic enclave, a so-called Koreatown, which is common in East and West Coast cities in the United States. Koreans in Minnesota have been scattered in almost all the suburbs around the Twin Cities area and have settled individually into their neighborhoods and business districts. Cities like Los Angeles and New York, with their densely populated Korean neighborhoods, have established Koreatowns that offer a whole variety of ethnic services, such as restaurants, grocery stores, hair salons, and leisure and entertainment facilities, including *Jjimjilbang* (Korean sauna) or *Norebang* (Korean karaoke).

The residential pattern of Koreans in Minnesota is widely scattered, lacking enough density in any area to form a Koreatown. In most major US cities, Korean ethnicity plays a major role in people's decisions about residence. Conversely, in Minnesota, occupation and job location, rather than ethnicity, seem to play a larger role. Many who arrived in Minnesota in the late 1960s were students and intellectuals studying at the University of Minnesota or other colleges. They tended to earn advanced degrees and settle in suburban areas in the south (e.g., Burnsville, Bloomington, Eagan, Cottage Grove) and west (Golden Valley, Plymouth, Maple Grove) after completing their studies and obtaining jobs. Many of the late-1970s and early-1980s Korean residents of these suburbs became engineers, white-collar employees working in major high-technology firms, such as Control Data, Honeywell, and Medtronic.[54]

Then, in Minnesota's Korean population of the mid-1970s, blue-collar workers started to outnumber professionals. Many of these blue-collar workers were highly educated professionals in Korea who lacked US credentials and found jobs in other industries. Others were relatives invited through chain immigration by early settlers and citizens, many of them married to Americans. Some of these Koreans started their own businesses: restaurants, grocery stores, billiard halls, hair salons, and video rental stores specializing in Korean TV shows and dramas opened between the 1980s and the early 1990s. As a handful of Korean ethnic stores began to operate along Snelling Avenue in St. Paul, the newly established Korean Chamber of Commerce supported the idea of building a Koreatown in that area.[55]

However, the plan to establish a Korean business district didn't succeed. Many of the 1980s immigrants found other employment, often in low-wage sectors. Unlike in major West Coast cities where jobs for Koreans are scarce but the Korean population is high, in Minnesota, Koreans didn't see much advantage in starting their own businesses upon arrival. As a result, the new Korean immigrants of the mid-1970s and 1980s arrived mainly in the northern Twin Cities suburbs of Fridley, New Brighton, and Brooklyn Park, locating especially around industrial plants, which became known as the "reception areas of new immigrants." Jobs in manufacturing and labor-intensive industries attracted these immigrants despite their higher educational background. Many of them brought substantial wealth and were able to purchase homes upon their arrival in these suburbs.[56]

With a diverse population ranging from students, educators, professionals, and interracial families to blue-collar workers, the Korean community emphasized the importance of a harmonious society—one that avoids many of

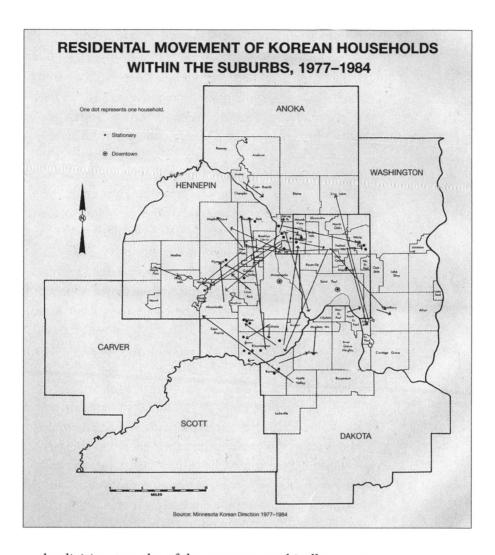

RESIDENTAL MOVEMENT OF KOREAN HOUSEHOLDS WITHIN THE SUBURBS, 1977–1984

One dot represents one household.

• Stationary

◉ Downtown

ANOKA

WASHINGTON

HENNEPIN

CARVER

SCOTT

DAKOTA

MILES

Source: Minnesota Korean Direction 1977–1984

the divisive struggles of the more geographically concentrated Korean communities on the West Coast. For example, the large influx of Koreans to Los Angeles in the mid-1980s led to a dense growth of Korean churches (from 319 protestant churches in 1982 to 649 in 2004). Many of the churches were established out of splits and struggles within the congregations, disrupting people's social networks and dividing the community in ways that prevented collaboration and unity.[57]

The Colorful Life of Today's Koreans in Minnesota

Snelling Avenue Korean Businesses. Despite the lack of a vibrant ethnic neighborhood near the Twin Cities' central business districts, quite a few Korean shops and service stores opened along Snelling Avenue in St. Paul. Today, new construction projects and property updates are constantly underway as most of the Snelling Avenue buildings date to the late nineteenth or early twentieth centuries. These few blocks have long been a popular area where one could easily find authentic Korean wares and services. Many Korean small businesses have been there for several decades.

One of the oldest Korean businesses in the Twin Cities area is Kim's Asian Market (previously Kim's Oriental Grocery), located at 689 Snelling Avenue North. Opened in 1975, the store was first owned by Ki Yong Kim. Kim had previously been a student at the University of Illinois and had worked as a data processor for Raymond Motors in Chicago, which later transferred him to the Twin Cities. When Raymond Motors shut down, Kim decided to go into business for himself. His initial investment was made with savings. Friends in the wholesale Asian import business gave him credit to buy their goods. In the early 1980s, the market really began to thrive. Customers include all Asian groups—Chinese, Japanese, Asian Indians, and Vietnamese. A sizeable influx of Hmong immigrants in the 1980s also increased demand for Asian foods. On weekends, Hmong people waited in long lines outside the store to buy rice. Today, Kim's market serves a diverse population but is still well known among Koreans as the oldest Korean grocery store in Minnesota.

Yeon Joo Cho (Lucia Kim) is the owner of Bella Beauty Salon, which opened in 1992 at 682 Snelling Avenue North. Cho and her husband, Ki Cheol Kim (Paul Kim), migrated to Minnesota in 1984. Her husband, born during the Korean War to an unmarried Korean mother and an American soldier father, led a challenged life in Korea because of his racial background. Ki Cheol's dream to start a new life with his family in the United States became a reality when he got a job at Ryerson Steel Company in Minnesota. While it was a difficult decision for Yeon Joo to drop her successful hair styling career in Korea, she knew what was best for her family. With the support and help of a Catholic priest under whom Ki Cheol Kim worked for a long time in Korea, the family opened a new chapter of their lives in Minnesota.

Another unique Korean spot is Sole Cafe, a restaurant that opened in the mid-1990s. The current owner, Kyongye Kim, came to the United States in 1972 as the fiancée of an American whom she married in Minnesota. She invited her sister, who became the first owner of Sole Cafe, in 1978. Kim took over the store in 1998. Kim is proud to serve Korean cuisine using only authentic homemade ingredients, such as *Doinjang* (soybean paste).

First joining 3M Korea in 1984, Hak Cheol Shin advanced in the company, serving multiple positions, including managing director of 3M Philippines in 1995. He was relocated to Minnesota with his family in 1997. "The change of climate from the tropical Philippines to the cold winter of Minnesota was most memorable when I arrived. . . . It was February, and there was 40 inches of snow on the ground. We didn't really know how to get around all that snow."

He continued his service in various areas, such as industrial and transportation business and later international operations. After twenty years of career advancement, Shin was appointed as vice chairman and executive vice president of the company.

During his early years in Minnesota, Shin struggled with many of the same issues most immigrants face—adapting to cultural changes and overcoming language barriers. "The first couple of years were tough. But I tried to keep things in perspective, especially trying to embrace my dual identity—one as a Korean back in my home country, but the other as an American here in the United States." Shin has been a board member of the Korean American Association of Minnesota, serving the Korean community in many ways. About thirty to forty Korean employees work at 3M, including some expatriates from Korea. After twenty-two years with the company, Shin returned to Korea to start a new leadership role as chief executive officer of LG Chemical.

Insun Hong (left) and Hak Cheol Shin at Insun Hong's retirement party, 2000

Nicole Johnson opened her business, Seoul Salon, in 2008 on Snelling Avenue. Adopted from Korea in 1983, Johnson has maintained a strong Korean identity through her involvement in the adoptee community. She is an active member of the Korean Cultural Association that is affiliated with Jang-mi Korean Dance and Drum and Korean Heritage House activities. The Heritage House was created in 1984 for Korean adoptees and their families to meet and celebrate Korean cultural heritage. Johnson's daughter performs with the Jang-mi Dance and Drum every year, and Johnson volunteers as much as she can. She is planning a visit to Korea with her daughter to meet her birth mother. She says, "I love being in the adoptee community because there are so many stories and connections. There is this unspoken kinship with the adoptees that can't be explained in words . . . the support, help, love, and compassion that is spread through the adoptee community is beautiful."

Yong Lee opened Mirror of Korea restaurant in May 1988; her son and daughter-in-law, Giok Choi, ran it for almost thirty years. In 2017, Changseung Yoo took over the restaurant, operating it with his mother. Despite the gradual decline of Snelling Avenue's Korean businesses, Yoo reports his restaurant, known as the most historic authentic Korean

Yeon Joo Cho at Bella Beauty Salon

restaurant in Minnesota, is doing fairly well: "We have been quite well connected to the Korean community. We've been asked to sponsor some events involving Korean adoptees, and also on occasions we've donated and catered Korean side dishes for special events organized by the Korean community."

These days, Korean ethnic stores are spread across Minnesota, including in Minneapolis, St. Paul, Chanhassen, Columbia Heights, Maplewood, Eagan, and Fridley. Many are located around the University of Minnesota campus to serve the Korean student population.

Nicole Johnson in front of Seoul Salon

Today, Minnesota's Korean population consists of a wide range of people—not just immigrants and adoptees but also international students, visiting scholars, and expatriates employed by various corporations. Members of these groups may not reside permanently in Minnesota, but they help the local community keep current with changes occurring back in Korea.

The Korean graduate and undergraduate student population at the University of Minnesota is itself critical in forming Korean student organizations and promoting a diverse campus culture. Korea ranked third in international student enrollment in the 2016–17 semester, with a total of 783 students. The UMN had the second-largest undergraduate Korean student population in Minnesota, and there were eighty-one Korean visiting scholars and sixteen Korean employees working at the UMN as researchers, clinicians, and faculty.[58]

The Future Korean Minnesotans

As Minnesota's population becomes increasingly diverse, Koreans in Minnesota are also becoming more diverse in their origins. Young, first-generation immigrants continue to arrive, drawn by the state's openness to different cultures and ethnicities, in addition to its main pull factor: numerous, high-quality educational establishments. Second- and third-generation Koreans are relatively free of the cultural and language barriers their parents and grandparents had to overcome. Unlike the early immigrants of the twentieth century, the new Korean immigrants of the twenty-first century will settle in a Minnesota with plenty of ethnic resources available for them and their children.

Twenty-first-century Korean immigrants in Minnesota differ from their predecessors. First, there are far fewer Korean adoptee children. The total number of Korean adoptees (age birth to seventeen) has dropped from 4,645 in 2000 to 1,265 between 2012–16. Almost 62 percent of the

Jang-mi Dance and Drum is a cultural school that offers classes in Korean traditional dancing and drumming. In 1984, a group of about twenty families hired Korean traditional dance teacher Ji-won Han. The group, which Han named "Jang-mi" or "Rose," met on Saturdays in a church for many years, then moved to a library and eventually into several different studio spaces.

When Han moved to California in 1997, Brooke Jee-in Newmaster, a member since its founding year, became the school's artistic director. Since then, Jang-mi's involvement in the local community has expanded substantially. Lessons are offered not only in St. Paul but also in Rochester, Minnesota, and Eau Claire, Wisconsin. In 2004, Jang-mi's first studio opened in North St. Paul, later relocating to St. Paul's Snelling Avenue near Kim's Market, Sole Cafe, and Mirror of Korea so students could visit the Korean store and restaurants every week. The studio, renamed the Korean Heritage House, offers a broad program of Korean cultural opportunities, including, for example, craft workshops using mulberry bark paper known as *hanji*. As a cultural center, the studio provides space for social gatherings, guest speakers, and performing artists.

A Korean adoptee herself, Newmaster grew up in Minnesota but always wanted to know more about her birth country. "Korean dance and drumming has given me a part of my identity that was lost growing up in a different culture from that of my birth. I feel very fortunate that I get to share Korea's beauty and art with others and hopefully help other Korean adoptees find pride in their roots." She hopes that learning Korean performance art will also build a stronger bond with other members of the Korean community and help them find their Korean identity.

Newmaster and the school have been major contributors to various events and activities immigrants have spent more than twenty-one years in the United States, with 33 percent of them reporting that they speak English well or very well. This is a major change from the 2000 immigrant population, in which only 26.6 percent reported having stayed more than twenty-one years and only 20.5 percent indicated that they speak English well or very well. In short, the newest Korean immigrants to Minnesota have more experience with and confidence in the American cultural experience and language than the immigrants of 2000. Over a relatively short period of time, the population has become increasingly "Americanized."[59]

Another change is in educational achievement. While the percentage of immigrants with a bachelor's degree has shown little change, there has been an increase of more than ten percentage points in people with advanced degrees. In 2000, 15.4 percent of the immigrants reported an advanced degree as their highest educational attainment, whereas 26.3 percent of the newest immigrants reported having an

celebrating Korean culture and heritage. Today, the classes consist of Korean adoptees, biracial Koreans, or children with Korean or Korean adopted parents, eager to learn the dances and music.

Newmaster is a passionate teacher and a respected leader in the Korean adoptee community. Besides running the school, Newmaster is also a board member of the Korean American Association, taking part in making decisions, organizing events, and connecting Korean immigrants with the adoptee community.[ix]

Jang-mi Dance and Drum 1987 recital

advanced degree. In contrast, those who reported them-selves as high school graduates only have also gone down ten percent, from 20.7 percent in 2000 to 10.8 between 2012–16. The increase of highly educated Korean immigrants indi-cates a potential "brain gain" to Minnesota.

There are also more homeowners among the newest immigrants. While 37.5 percent of the immigrants owned a home in 2000, the homeowner population sharply in-creased to 57.4 percent between 2012–16. The median household income also went up, from $41,777 to $60,587. The new Korean immigrants are substantially wealthier and economically more stable. In contrast, the income gap between the rich and the poor has widened. While 8.6 percent of the Korean immigrants in 2000 were reported below the poverty line, this portion of the population has increased almost five percent, to 13.3 percent among the newest immigrants. While representing only a small per-centage of the overall population, the growth of inequality within the Korean community suggests potential margin-alization of the poor.[60]

The future Korean Minnesotans will easily blend into American society and culture and may have less concern over their Korean identity. Consequently, some believe there may be a weaker sense of ethnic solidarity, as many will have limited need to rely on the Korean community to receive services and information or build social networks. Some may call Korean professionals in the immigrant com-munity the "do-nothing class," raising concerns that these intellectuals are more self-interested and will "even forget that they are descendants of Koreans."[61]

However, Koreans in Minnesota are hardly neglect-ing their cultural heritage. Despite concerns about weak-ening bonds, the next two sections—on the history of Korean churches and building the Korean community—demonstrate an eagerness to band together and continue to provide resources for all Koreans in Minnesota.

Korean Churches in Minnesota

Generally, Koreans are known for their strong ethnic attachment and solidarity. Aside from racial and cultural unity, Korean Americans in the United States share a unique history of Christianity that has led to the significant growth and influence of Korean ethnic churches within the immigrant community. Among the seven thousand early Korean immigrants in Hawaii, more than four hundred were already baptized Christians before they arrived. And within only ten years, Korean Christians made up about 40 percent of the total Korean population in Hawaii. Since then, in Korean immigrant communities the church has been a focal point of many activities and gatherings. Beyond offering religious and spiritual guidance, the church has provided a place of "ethnic fellowship," promoting Korean ethnic identity that helps preserve cultural traditions and social customs.[62]

To understand the dynamics of Korean immigrant life in Minnesota, it is necessary to look into how Korean ethnic churches were formed, expanded, separated, and continued to grow. Currently, there are about fourteen Korean churches in Minnesota.

The Evangelical Churches

The root of the various evangelical churches started with a Bible study group formed among a small number of Christian Korean graduate students at the University of Minnesota in 1959. Bo Eun Kim, a graduate student of hospital administration who also happened to be a Presbyterian church elder in Korea, was the group's first leader. Other active members in the early years included Yoon Bum Kim, a physician and graduate student in microbiology; Joo Ho Sung, an assistant professor in neuropathology at the UMN Medical School; and Yun Ho Lee, the owner of Lee's

Apron Manufacturing Company. Each Sunday afternoon the group met at the United Campus Christian Fellowship on the university's St. Paul campus. Sometimes, the group also invited guest speakers, usually American ministers. The Bible study group grew steadily, also welcoming newcomers and visitors to share information and to provide a place to mingle and interact.

In 1967, as the Bible study group continued to grow, five young Presbyterian ministers came from Korea to study at the Central Baptist Theological Seminary in Minneapolis, where Chang Yub Kim (Daniel Kim), a Korean professor, was teaching. The ministers suggested the Bible study group should become an actual church and proposed a committee be set up to start the process. As a result, within a year, under the leadership of Professor Kim, the Bible study group became a more formal organization: the Korean Christian Fellowship (KCF). To preserve the unity of the Korean community, the interdenominational organization used the term *fellowship* to encourage the inclusion of non-Christians into its fold. In this way the fellowship would serve as a transition between the Bible study group and an official church.

The fellowship's first service was held at the United Campus Christian Fellowship on the university's Minneapolis campus in July 1968. The service was attended by about ninety people, which was about two-thirds of the Koreans living in the Twin Cities at that time. Several months later, the fellowship began holding meetings at the Weyerhaeuser Chapel at Macalester College, and Chang Yub Kim became senior pastor. From 1968 to 1972, KCF was the religious center of the Korean community, but it also provided a space for cultural and social activities. One of its major initiatives was teaching immigrant children Korean language and culture after Sunday school.

As the fellowship continued to grow, some members felt it was time to change it into a traditional church. Chang

Korean Christian Fellowship's first gathering at the University of Minnesota, July 1968: bottom row, left to right, Dr. Juhn (UMN), Dr. Ko (Korean Medical School), Dr. Joo Ho Sung (UMN Medical School), Yun Ho Lee, Dr. H. Hahn (Korea), Rev. S. Lee, Rev. Daniel Kim, Mrs. Daniel Kim, Rev. T. Kim, Rev. Y. Chang (Christian minister, Taegu, Korea); left in the second row from the bottom: Dr. Yoon Bum Kim

Yub Kim, who was followed mainly by those who had recently arrived in Minnesota, supported the idea of a traditional church and pressed for a denominational affiliation. However, the early founding members were against the idea, fearing that an official church would divide the community. They advocated for the fellowship to remain a separate entity.

Several months later, in 1971, the fellowship split into two groups, one forming the Korean Church of the Twin Cities (KCTC), and the other continuing the fellowship under the leadership of its charter members, including Yun Ho Lee, Joo Ho Sung, Changwon Song, a professor in radiology at the University of Minnesota Medical School, and Hyun Sang Cha, a Methodist seminarian and social worker.

In 1975, KCTC underwent another split, with a group leaving to form the Korean United Methodist Church

(KUMC), which located in Oakdale in 1976. After two years, the Methodist church purchased a school building in New Brighton and renovated the gym to be used as the main chapel. In 1986, the church had about three hundred members. Yung Lyun Ko, one of KUMC's original members, recalls the Methodist church being more popular among blue-collar workers as opposed to KCF, which was mostly attended by professionals. In 1978, there was yet another split within KCTC, which disbanded when Chang Yub Kim left and formed the Korean First Baptist Church (KFBC); the other group formed the Korean Presbyterian Church of the Twin Cities (KPCTC).[63]

In the meantime, the Korean Christian Fellowship continued to serve its members, and in 1973 it called Seo Young Baik, a Korean Methodist from Colorado, to serve as pastor. The fellowship went through several location changes, from the Bethany Baptist Church in Roseville, to the St. Anthony Park United Methodist Church, and finally into an old Presbyterian church in Minneapolis.

In 1975, KCF became an official, but interdenominational, church renamed as the Korean Community Church

Korean Christian Fellowship language school and Sunday school, 1972

(KCC) of Minnesota; in 1977 it settled in the chapel of the Hennepin Avenue United Methodist Church. But soon, Reverend Baik suggested that the congregation should join the United Methodist Church Conference. When his request was voted down, he broke away from KCC, taking his own and a few more followers to form the Korean Evangelical United Methodist Church (KEUMC) in 1979. KEUMC had its first Sunday service in Oakdale and later worshipped in Fridley.[64]

KCC had several pastors serving the congregation, including Jin Saeng Jung, a retired Presbyterian minister from Korea, and Heui Seong Gil, a seminarian and assistant professor at St. Olaf College. Finally, in March 1980, Presbyterian minister Young Jae Kim arrived from West Germany to serve as pastor. Under his leadership, the congregation doubled its size to eighty adults and forty Korean children enrolled in Sunday school, but its growth was slow compared to the other Korean churches.[65]

KCC, even with its fellowship mission, was primarily perceived as a church among the earlier settlers. But as the Korean population continued to grow, more recent arrivals sought a more traditional Korean-style church, and the original vision of KCC as a church focused on being the social center of learning the American way of life did not attract many newcomers. To cope with these challenges, in 1981 the congregation chose a Presbyterian denomination and changed its name to Korean First Church of Minnesota (KFCM).[66]

Although these congregations went their separate ways, they also maintained close relationships in working together toward a unified Korean community. A music worship service celebrating Christmas was held in the KPCTC in 1978, with all four churches contributing to the special program. Each pastor took part in the service. The Catholic church also made an appearance in the program as a special guest.[67]

KPCTC, which broke from KCTC in 1978, maintained its presence along with KFCM for about ten years. But in 1990, both churches recognized the need to create a single Korean Presbyterian church and started negotiating a unification process. In July 1990, a joint special service brought the two churches closer together, and in August, both pastors gave their sermons in front of their counterpart's congregants. A contentious issue was the location of the chapel. KPCTC's members wanted to retain their current building as the chapel once the two groups were unified, whereas KFCM's members wanted a new place of worship. After a series of negotiations, the committee reached an agreement and successfully purchased a new chapel in its current location in Brooklyn Center under the name of the Korean Presbyterian Church of Minnesota (KPCM).[68]

In 2004, the English congregation of KPCM, mostly consisting of one-and-a half- and second-generation Korean Americans, formed a multicultural church: Church of All Nations. Initially renting the space of a nearby declining white Presbyterian church, the congregation merged with the Shiloh Bethany Presbyterian church, which was dissolving. The timely union would serve an increasingly multicultural population in Columbia Heights—and it continues to do so today.[69]

In addition to the churches that broke out of the Korean Christian Fellowship of 1968, a few small churches were independently established in the 1980s, including the Seventh-day Adventist Church and the Grace Korean Church.

The Seventh-day Adventist Church was officially established in May 1980 by Reverend Byung Hoon Shin. A few faithful families, including Choong Sik Kim and his relatives, began to gather in 1979, and a year later, the church was officially organized. In 1986, sixty people were members. Today, the church is located in Minneapolis under the name of Minneapolis Korean Church.[70]

Grace Korean Church was at first named Minnesota Full Gospel Church. The congregation held its first worship service in 1981 with about twenty-five members. Several pastors served and left the church, until in 1986, under the leadership of Pastor Sang Joo Goh, the church officially changed its

First unified Presbyterian church service, 1991: left to right, Chong Hae Jung, Yun Ho Lee, Young Ho Kang

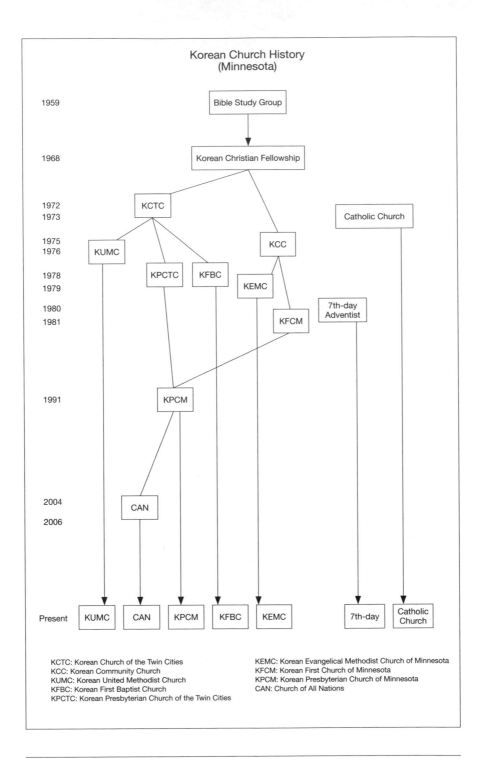

Korean Church History
(Minnesota)

1959 — Bible Study Group

1968 — Korean Christian Fellowship

1972 / 1973 — KCTC

Catholic Church

1975 / 1976 — KUMC, KCC

1978 / 1979 — KPCTC, KFBC, KEMC

1980 / 1981 — KFCM, 7th-day Adventist

1991 — KPCM

2004 / 2006 — CAN

Present — KUMC, CAN, KPCM, KFBC, KEMC, 7th-day, Catholic Church

KCTC: Korean Church of the Twin Cities
KCC: Korean Community Church
KUMC: Korean United Methodist Church
KFBC: Korean First Baptist Church
KPCTC: Korean Presbyterian Church of the Twin Cities

KEMC: Korean Evangelical Methodist Church of Minnesota
KFCM: Korean First Church of Minnesota
KPCM: Korean Presbyterian Church of Minnesota
CAN: Church of All Nations

name to Grace Korean Church. About forty members gathered for its second opening worship service.[71]

Currently, about thirteen Korean evangelical churches, including the Korean Seventh-day Adventist Church, serve the community.

The Catholic Church

Unlike the evangelical Korean churches in Minnesota, the Korean Catholic church has maintained a single church community since it was officially established in 1974. Before that, believers gathered in small groups under the leadership of Deacon Min Soo (Timothy) Kim. Soon the faithful sought to have regular meetings and, in 1973, formed an executive committee to organize an official Catholic church. A year later, on April 16, 1974, with Reverend Francis Choe (Chi Kyu) leading the congregation, the new church was officially recognized by the Archdiocese of St. Paul–Minneapolis as the Catholic Church of the Korean Community of the Twin Cities. Since most of the congregants were students, the Korean Catholic church became part of the St. Lawrence Newman Center at the University of Minnesota. The early core members included Deacon Kim, Michael (Kangui) Hong, Joseph (Chang Jae) Lee, Andrea (Kyun) Huh, Maria (Hyunsil) Chang, and nuns Stephanan Choong and Yuriana Choe. Reverend Choe was officially designated as the church's pastor in 1975.[72]

Over the next decade, the Catholic church thrived as the congregation grew and organized outreach events. In May 1975, the church arranged a panel discussion on human rights in Korea. In 1977, the church's baseball and volleyball teams each won first place at a sporting event hosted by the Korean American Association of Minnesota. As membership increased, the church established a building fund. In the meantime, Cardinal Stephano Kim visited from Korea and baptized twenty-two members and confirmed seventeen.

Several church leaders celebrated academic achievements, including Reverend Choe with a bachelor's degree in psychology from St. Thomas and Sister Choong with a doctoral degree in plant physiology. Reverend Choe and Sister Choong were among the earliest and most dedicated members in establishing and consolidating the Korean Catholic community.

Even as the congregation grew and continued to organize various religious and social activities, it didn't have its own place to worship. Then, in 1979, the community's longtime wish for its own building came true when the church

Chang Jae (Joseph) Lee is a retired deacon of the St. Andrew Kim Church. A founding member of the early Korean Catholic community in Minnesota, he served two terms as its leader. Lee came to Minnesota with his family in 1973. He had been involved in the April 19, 1960, student revolution that toppled the authoritarian First Republic of South Korea. While working as a congressional correspondent for Daegu's major daily newspaper, he innocently became involved in yet another political incident that led him to resign from his post. He intended to apply for political asylum in the United States, but because his wife is a doctor, he was able to take advantage of immigration preferences. With the help of Dr. Changwon Song, a professor of radiology at the University of Minnesota who arranged a residency for Lee's wife, Chung Kyu Kin Lee, his family found their home in Minnesota.

Lee continued to work toward democracy for South Korea—a movement that was promoted across the United States by like-minded Koreans.

Chang Jae Lee

News of his arrival inspired the political activist community to continue fighting. He served as a representative of the Korean Democratic Revolutionary Party that was formed in early 1979 in Washington, DC. However, when Park Chung-hee, the president of South Korea, was assassinated and the government removed by a military coup, Lee gave up his dreams of returning to Korea to assist in establishing democratic leadership.

His desperation turned into hope when he was spiritually reborn in 1980 and designated as a permanent deacon of the Minnesota Korean Catholic Church by the archbishop of St. Paul and Minneapolis in 1986.

moved to 580 Case Avenue in St. Paul. The first mass in the new church building was held on Christmas Eve.

The church engaged actively with its new neighbors. In May 1980, for example, it participated in the annual Wilder Community Festival by introducing Korean cultures to attendees. An open house event in July 1981 was specifically aimed at promoting Korean cultures and arts to people in the area. The congregation hoped to improve community relations, especially since the church building had been targeted by vandalism.[73]

In 1986, the church moved its chapel to Corpus Christi in North St. Paul and officially changed its name to Church of St. Andrew Kim Catholic Church. Currently, the parish holds masses at the Church of the Holy Childhood in St. Paul.

Catholic church of the Korean Community, 580 Case Avenue, St. Paul, 1981

Building a Korean Community

The Korean community of Minnesota began as an academic network, mostly made up of students attending the University of Minnesota. Over time, however, the population became more diverse as migrants of various professions and backgrounds arrived in the state. Minnesota's Koreans have promoted connections between individuals and families by organizing social groups and establishing formal institutions that celebrate Korean culture.

Strengthening and Uniting Korean Americans: The Korean American Association of Minnesota

One of the state's oldest Korean organizations is the Korean American Association of Minnesota (KAAM), which began as a campus group at the University of Minnesota in 1954, mainly under the leadership of Yun Ho Lee, a graduate student and later a business owner. Its other leader was Joo Ho Sung, an assistant professor of neuropathology at the UMN Medical School in 1962. Lee served as the president of the association from 1954 to 1964, and Sung took over for two years after that. Many faculty members arrived from Seoul National University through the exchange program. In the 1960s and 1970s, more Koreans arrived, leading to growth of the association and of the immigrant population in general.

There were some challenges. A certain tension existed between KAAM members who were settling in the community and the students in the Korean Student Association (KSA), formed in 1955. KSA was more progressive, but some people were involved with both organizations. KAAM, led by the early arrivals and their families, supported the students by providing transportation to events and inviting them for Korean meals and opportunities to cook outside the university's residence halls. Close connections between the two organizations started to deteriorate as more students arrived in the mid-1960s and many of the earlier students left upon graduation.

However, in 1970 the two groups set aside their differences and united as Koreans in Minnesota by participating in the Minneapolis Aquatennial. The theme was "Seas of the Orient," and Korean immigrants contributed floats, craft exhibits, dance performances, finger foods, and taekwondo demonstrations. This was the first time the entire Korean community participated in a major Minnesota-wide event, and its success drew members closer together.[74]

It was also in 1970 that KAAM and KSA created *The Kernel: A Korean Community Newsletter in Minnesota.* This four-page publication was divided into sections of interest to Koreans: current politics and economics in Korea; news on local events; and information about people who married, had children, graduated, or left the area. Sometimes the newsletter featured recipes of popular, traditional Korean foods and poetry and short stories written by local Koreans.

Beginning in the mid-1970s, an increase in the Korean population led to the growth of smaller organizations and social groups. As participation in and cooperation with KAAM began to weaken, there were serious talks about shutting it down. Some believed its continuation would only create more conflict among those who volunteered most of their time to keep it afloat. In 1976, the association was on the verge of being dissolved—until new leadership introduced a fresh approach. President Myung Choon Park and administrative director Shin Heng Huh had some ideas for improvement. In 1976, Huh relaunched *The Kernel* as the *Korean Newsletter,* an important source of community information, covering both major events and daily happenings for local Koreans. The newsletter also published the names of people who donated even one dollar to the association to show appreciation for their support. In

Korean American Association members and Aquatennial organizers, Queen Annette, beauty pageant winner, and Chicago Korean consul general, 1970

about a month, the association collected $621, which was enough to keep the *Korean Newsletter* running.[75]

In July 1976, the association once again participated in the Minneapolis Aquatennial, setting up a major Korean exhibition. Despite the rainy weather, members went above and beyond, engaging in friendly competitions with the Chinese and Japanese community. KAAM didn't stop there. That October, a series of "Minnesota Korean Day" events were launched at the University of Minnesota's St. Paul campus, including a public panel that invited prominent Korean scholars from other states to discuss international affairs and South-North Korean relations.[76]

The heyday of KAAM was in 1978, when Minnesota governor Rudy Perpich declared "Korean Day" in October in recognition of the annual "Minnesota Korean Day" celebrations that KAAM had organized for years. Governor Perpich noted that "through such annual celebrations can be created a spirit of fraternalism and pride amongst our people for their heritage and recognition of the fact that

제 1 호
（창간호）
1971년 1월 1일

씨 알

발행인: 한국인회및학생회
편집인: 서 정 우
편집소: 3020 East 25th St.
Mpls., Minn. 55406

The Kernel, a Korean Community Newsletter in Minnesota

═내나라소식

정치

금년 대통령 선거 준비 작업의 하나로 정당한 내각이 물러나고 백두진씨를 중심으로 한 새 내각이 구성. 공화당의 주도권도 김종필씨를 중심으로 다시 재편성되었다.

유엔 총회는 지난 12월 7일에 한국 통일 결의안을 찬성 67, 반대 28, 그리고 기권 22표로 승인했다. 이 통한 결의안의 중요 골자는 주한 외국군의 계속 주둔과 인권과의 주한 활동 계속 등이다.

× × ×

1969년 11월부터 공화, 신민 양당 간에서 시작된 선거법 개정협상이 1년여 만에 매듭을 짓고 지난 12월 16일 3개 선거 법 개정안이 국회 본회의에서 통과 됐다. 그 중요한 골자는 ① 유령투표 방지를 또렷한 투표, 개표 부정의 방지, ② 부정의 관권 개제 ③ 선거운동 규제 조항의 완화 등이다.

× × ×

경제

소위 "빈즈밤인"이 지난 11월 19일 미 하원에서 215대 165 표로 가결 통과되었다. 이 법안이 상원을 통과, 대통령의 서명으로 법률화된다면 한국을 비롯한 일본, 대만, 홍콩 등의 대미 피륙 수출에 상당한 영향이 미쳐질 것으로 보인다.

× × ×

사회

서울 형사 지법은 지난 12월 4일에 마약 밀매 혐자 부부 살해사건 관련 홍한 씨 등 강도의 공소 사실을 모두 유죄로 인정, 이란 두 변사에게 사형 선고를 내렸다. 이 두 피고는 마약을 팔지 않았다고 한국인 부부를 죽이고 또한 어린아이 남매 등도 도망했다고 한다.

× × ×

부산과 제주도 사이를 왕래하던 "남영호" 연락선이 지난 12월 15일에 부산 근해에서 효과 인원과 화물 적재로 침몰하여 약 330명 가량이 사망했다.

× × ×

문화

1973년부터 현실하려던 정부의 한글 전용 방침이 명확한 반대에 부디쳐 수정될지도 모른다는 관측.

× × ×

스포츠

타이랜드 수도 방콕에서 열렸던 제6회 아시아 경기대회에서 한국은 종합 전적 제2위로 금메달 18개, 은메달 13개, 그리고 동메달 23개를 획득했다. 1위인 은 본이고 3위는 이란이다.

여러분께 세배를 드립니다

씨알을 축하하며

미네소다 한국인회 및 학생회에서 "씨알"이란 신문을 발행하게 된 것은 무한히 기쁘게 생각하며 이 신 기관지인 사업을 시작하기 위하여 노력하신 여러분들의 수고에 대하여 진심으로 감사의 뜻을 표하는 바이며 금후 여회 기획한 사업이 알찬 발전하기를 기원하는 바입니다.

"씨알" 제1호 발행을 기하여 한국인 한 사람으로서 바라는 바는 우리들이 협심협력하여 미네소다 한국인 지역 사회를 발전시키는 동시에 항상 화목하게 지내자는 것입니다. 지난 7월에 거행된 "아파 해니알" 행사시에 우리들이 보인 봉사적 이고 애국하는 정신과 자라가 인정하는 바이며 이러한 정신이 계속 보지되어 더 발전된 한국인 사회가 형성될기를 바라는 바 입니다. 그러면 금후 어떻게 하는것이 보범하게 사회를 이루는데 좋은 제물 볼까요. 들으면 저는 다음 두 가지를 원하고 싶습니다.

첫째로, 한국인 모임과 교회나 일에 개방적 이어야 하며 기타 사업에 지장이 없는 한 가급적 참석하도록 노력하는 것 입니다.

둘째로, 민족의 "아이덴티디"를 잊지 않는 것입니다. 우리는 새로운 문화에 동화되기 쉬운 좋은 특성을 가지고 있으나 이 반면에 쉽게 민족의 "아이덴티디"를 잊기 위금 단점도 갖었으나 있습니다. 유태인이 2천여년이 나 나라 없이 해외에서 생활 했지만 1948년에는 다시 자기네 나라를 찾을수 있었다는 이 정신은 우리들은 본 받아 각자가 노력합시다. 신년에도 회원 제위의 건강과 소원의 성취되기를 바랍니다. [이 윤호]

창 간 사

한국 사람이 이 고장에 언제 처음으로 발을 부치었느지는 모르나 언제려 기 시작한 것은 적어도 20년이 넘음을 압니다. 모든 우리의 수도 400명을 넘으며 우리도 이 사회에서 소수이기는 하나 한 지역사회의 면모를 갖추어 할 때가 된 것입니다. 이 때에 우리가 바라던 Newsletter가 창간하게 된 것은 당연한 일이며, 우리 한인사회 회의 발전을 돕는 다면하는 것이 아닐 수 없어, 우리가 다 같이 축하 하여 야 할 경사인 것 입니다.

모든 가치 있는 사업들이 그렇듯이 1971년 첫날을 기해서 창간이 이 신문도 결코 우연의 산물이 아닌것을 여러분들에게 출즘드리고자 바라 다. 회원수가 많아 감에 따라 어떤 형태의 신문이 절실히 필요하다는 것을 느끼게 된 것입니다. 지난 여름에 우리가 "씨에미나"에서 그 필요성이 심각히 논의되었던 것이니 다. 한국인회 임원회에서 재정 감사의 되었고 위원회에서는 이 신문의 발전을 한인회의 중요한 사업중의 하나로 인정하므로 그 운영비를 예산으로 책정함으로서 그 기초가 마련된 것입니다.

이에 따라 문화부장이 이런여지 로 신문화에 조예가 깊고 열성적인 협조를 자청하여 주신 선우홍균, 서정우 그리고 신은희의 많이 상의 하여 편집위원회를 마련하고 서정우씨 를 편집인으로 추대함으로서 이 신문의 발족을 선언하게 된것 입니다.

이 분들의 헌신적인 노력도 더 말할바 없거니와 그 외에도 음양으로 협조를 아끼지 않으신 여러분에게 충심으로 감사를 드리는 바 입니다. 오늘 발족한 이 신문을 편집하려 수 결선분들의 협력을 예약하지만 법명하지도 활발있음 것이며 회원 여러분들이 아낌없이 협조하여 주시고 추천 하여 주생보을 믿는 바입니다.

앞으로 이 신문이 우리 회원 상호간의 이해를 촉진하고 화목을 증진하는 매개체가 되고 우리 한인 사회의 건실한 발전의 희망이 되어 주었으면 하는 것은 비단 본인만의 염원이 아니겠습니다. [서우호]

◎ 윤호선생의 **에프론제조회사**는 한국 여자 종업원 약간명을 채용한다고 합니다. 일하실 의사가 계시면 전화 788-6905로 연락바람
※ 이선생님개인적 변상으로 회원에 100불을 협사하였습니다.

First edition of *The Kernel: A Korean Community Newsletter in Minnesota* such spirit has much to offer America in the years to come." KAAM had campaigned to have an official day celebrating the spirit of the Korean community in Minnesota. Ever since, the first Saturday of October is officially designated as "Korean Day."[77]

Other major accomplishments of KAAM include the successful efforts to have a Korean flag hung at the Minneapolis–St. Paul International Airport. The airport's policy was to only permit the flags of United Nations countries. After repeated requests to make an exception, the Korean flag was hung as the 156th flag of a foreign country on display at the airport.[78]

When Korea announced it was to be the host country of the 1988 Summer Olympics, KAAM worked with the Minnesota Zoo to send two purebred Siberian tigers to Korea in June 1986 in exchange for two white cranes.[79]

Today, KAAM is the overarching organization that launches major activities for Korean Americans and sponsors and supports other Korean-related activities. Annual events include the Festival of Nations in May, at which KAAM sells Korean food and sets up a display of Korean culture and history. At two annual visits of the Korean consulate in Chicago, in May and October, KAAM coordinates to assist Minnesota Koreans with passport or immigration-related paperwork.

Korean Independence Day, on August 15, has tremendous meaning for the Korean immigrant community. To celebrate the Korean national holiday and instill pride in and awareness of Korean identity, KAAM hosts a series of events around that time, including writing and drawing contests for children.

Once a year in September, the Korean community gathers on a large scale to participate in an all-day sporting event that includes soccer and volleyball. While hosted by KAAM, it is also an event at which the church community comes together for a picnic-style meal.

Members of the Korean American Association with Governor Rudy Perpich signing the Proclamation of Korean Day, October 3, 1978

KAAM has its own Korean language school with about thirty second- and third-generation Korean children enrolling each semester. As a fund-raiser, the school organizes a bazaar to sell Korean dishes.

In 2016, after thirty-seven years of continuous effort to find a permanent location for its functions and administration, KAAM purchased its own office space in Vadnais Heights. Currently, it is also raising funds to build a Korean Cultural Center for future generations of Koreans in Minnesota.[80]

A Korean Education and Cultural Center: The Korean Institute of Minnesota

Beginning in the mid-1970s, as more Koreans started to arrive and settle in various areas of Minnesota, demand for a Korean resource center was rising. In 1974, Tae Hwan Kim, Changwon Song, Sung Kyun Chun, and Yung Lyun Ko, among like-minded others, founded the Korean Institute of Minnesota (KIM) with about $10,000 generously donated by community members. On its inaugural day in March 1975, more than two hundred people participated in the opening ceremony.[81]

The goal was mainly to educate second-generation Korean American children in their cultural heritage and language, but KIM also offered classes in traditional dancing, cooking, and taekwondo. Traditional Korean songs were taught, and cookbooks were sold for donations. Many immigrant parents were afraid that their children, mostly born in the United States, would eventually lose their connection with their native culture and their Korean language skills. While several Korean churches were already running language schools, Dr. Tae Hwan Kim convinced them to dissolve their classes and unify under KIM.

Interestingly, despite its initial aim to serve American-born Korean children, the language school of KIM became more popular among Korean adoptees. At the first meeting, at the Urban West Central YMCA in Minneapolis, about eighty adopted Korean children and their parents came. As the number of attendees grew dramatically, the organization moved out of the YMCA, using the building of Seward Elementary School in Minneapolis instead. Over the next several years, KIM engaged in various fundraising efforts, including silent auctions and performances of traditional Korean songs and dances. To the adoptees' parents, KIM's message—"when you adopt a Korean child, you adopt Korean culture"—was powerful, prompting generous purchases, such as valuable works of Korean calligraphy. Besides history and culture, children also learned Korean dances and paper folding, as well as taekwondo. Parents could learn Korean cooking and take Korean painting classes.[82]

Since its founding, the institute has served as a valuable resource center for many people with links to Korea, including Minnesota families who adopted Korean children.

With approximately fifteen thousand children adopted from Korea in Minnesota, KIM prides itself on playing a vital role in connecting the community with adoptees. Especially for those who have multiple identities—as a Korean, an American, and an adoptee—KIM offers a place for both children and their parents to understand Korean cultural heritage and to help pass it on to the next generation. KIM activities and celebrations allow for the sharing of Korean identity.[83]

Korean flag song performance at the Korean Institute, Minneapolis, 1975

Currently, KIM's eleven teachers work with more than sixty students each semester. The institute welcomes a significant Korean adoptee population in all classes, ranging from prekindergarten to adult. The students' parents are also diverse, including in their number Korean adoptees or racially mixed parents and adults not of Korean heritage but who are interested in learning Korean.

Other than language courses, the institute holds in-class cultural events that coincide with Korean holidays, such as *Choosuk*, Korean Thanksgiving day, at which students participate in traditional folk games like *Jeggichagi*.

Korean Institute
language and cul-
ture program, year-
end picnic, 1980

Also, traditional foods, such as *paddbingsoo*, a red bean shaved-ice dessert, are made at the beginning of the fall semester to introduce students to a staple summer snack.[84]

Minnesota Korean Elder Association

After the Immigration Act of 1965 expanded opportunities to students, professionals, and family members, many elderly Koreans were invited over by their children who were already settled in Minnesota. However, the euphoria of seeing their children and the excitement and hopes of a new life in the United States quickly evaporated as they were faced with limited mobility, language barriers, and longing for their much more active lives back in Korea. Only after becoming a foreigner did they truly feel the warmth of their home country.

Despite the challenges, some engaged in serving the immigrant community and some obtained jobs, while others enjoyed spending time with their grandchildren. Some also moved to assisted living quarters for more independence. For many elders, church became a place to meet and socialize with fellow Koreans.[85]

These older immigrants valued these personal connections, and finally in September 1978 about thirty elders gathered at the International Institute of Minnesota and held the first official meeting of the Korean Elder Association (KEA). By the mid-1980s, membership grew to more than 150, and by 1998, 220 people were members of the association.[86]

KEA did more than provide social gatherings of fellow Korean elders; its members actively engaged in promoting Korean culture and traditions and in educating the community on Korean political and social issues. They hosted a variety of panel discussions with guest speakers, organized social events, and created an award for those whose good deeds were recognized by the community.

KEA was disbanded in 2000, but it left a legacy of bridging generations and drawing those who could have been lonely or disconnected into active and significant roles in the community.

From Korean Wives to Korean Women: Korean American Women's Association

One of the first groups of Koreans to immigrate to Minnesota were Korean women married to American servicemen. Many of these women moved to the United States after the Korean War with little understanding of how their lives would be in their new home. They were among the earliest Koreans to arrive in the United States, but they were scattered around the country mostly in small towns and therefore had limited interactions with other Koreans. In the early 1980s, many began to band together to build their own community.

"There weren't many Koreans in Minneapolis and St. Paul area and we were yearning for friends and family back in home. Above all what we missed most was the Korean food that we used to eat. Because of that, when they run into Korean people, they were bonded instantaneously and easily built a friendship," recalls Kapsun Adams, who served as president of the Korean American Women's Association (KAWA) in 1994. Kim Hanson, an early member of the association who came to the United States in 1957, made traditional Korean soy bean soup with soy bean paste her mother had shipped from Korea. She recalled that it was "just like eating precious honey." With neither Korean grocery stores nor Korean restaurants available, eating food that reminded these women of home was an emotional experience.[87]

This longing and the instant bonding over food and culture brought these women together in their homes to share Korean meals and their life stories. As word of these gatherings spread, more and more women wanted to join. The informal group decided to create a more organized and structured institution to share the benefits with more local Korean women.

In August 1981, about thirty members gathered to officially launch the Korean American Wives Association. Since its founding, the organization has been actively engaged in supporting and participating in events like the Festival of Nations, projects for the Korean Service Center, Korean Culture Camp activities, and many more. In 2002, the organization was renamed the Korean American Women's Association to broaden its membership to all Korean women, not just those who came to the United States through international marriages. From 2010 to 2012, under the leadership of Kuncha Johnson, the association actively recruited members in the Eau Claire, Wisconsin, area.

In 2005, KAWA joined the national Korean American Women's Association, based in Washington, DC. Members of Minnesota's KAWA have served in various administrative positions for the larger group. JinHee Darmer, who served as president of the local Minnesota KAWA in 2003, led the initiative to take the Minnesota chapter to the national level.

What started as a small friendship group is today one of the most active and self-sufficient institutions in the Korean community. Its mission is to empower women not only as the primary caretakers of their families but also as bridges joining American and Korean cultures.

Providing Social Services to Koreans: The Korean Service Center

The need to establish a social services center was first recognized by Grace Lee, the founder and first executive director of the Korean Service Center (KSC). Lee immigrated to Hibbing, Minnesota, in 1953, and was married to the town doctor, William Lee. While she was teaching English language classes for Korean American elders in 1986, she also volunteered as a liaison between the Korean community and the Minneapolis Public Housing Authority. About sixty Korean seniors were living in the four buildings of the Cedars apartment complex in south Minneapolis, and they had problems adjusting to US culture. Lee began to help them with their daily frustrations, including their feelings of isolation because they couldn't speak the language. "To the Americans, the Koreans seemed unfriendly. The Koreans, on the other hand, felt that the Americans didn't like them.... [I]t's really fun now to watch the Korean[s] say 'hello' in English and then watch the residents say 'hello' back. They all smile, and it makes a huge difference," said Diane Levitt, a social worker for senior resources. In Lee's classes, the elders learned English and received help completing forms for medical assistance, rent refund, and other services. Lee's role was critical in reducing tensions and bridging the cultural gap.[88]

Members of the Korean American Women's Association and the Korean American Association of Minnesota at the Festival of Nations, 2018

In 1989, Lee met Dr. Ailee Moon, a professor at the graduate school of social work at the University of Minnesota, and together they developed the idea of creating a bilingual and bicultural service center for Korean immigrants. The effort involved county senior service officials, senior resource staff, and Korean community leaders, who were supportive of the idea of a nonprofit social service agency for Koreans. As a result, in June 1990, the Minnesota Korean American Multi Service Center—renamed the Korean Service Center (KSC) in 1992—was launched.[89]

Yunjoo Park has been the executive director of KSC since 1995. She immigrated to Minnesota in 1975 along with her husband, who studied for his MBA at the University of Minnesota. Park earned a degree in education and worked at Catholic Charities as a Korean adoption social worker. She remembers two major KSC accomplishments that brought the organization into public light. One inspiring event took place in September 1995, when 106 Koreans (mostly elders) became naturalized in a special ceremony supported by Senator Paul Wellstone. Prior to the ceremony, immigration officers came directly to KSC for two days to prepare applicants and assist them in completing their civics tests and interviews. The oath ceremony set the record as having naturalized the largest single ethnic group in Minnesota history.[90]

Also, in 2000, KSC organized a rally to protest the construction of a light rail transit line that would force KSC to move a decade-old vegetable garden located near I-94 and Cedar Avenue in Minneapolis. The Minneapolis Community Development Agency had granted a garden permit for the lot, and city workers plowed the land and let the Korean seniors use water from a nearby hydrant. Soon, about forty Koreans started to produce turnips, zucchini, sesame plants, onions, and hot peppers and chives. The garden had become an unofficial Korean cultural center, a therapeutic place for elders who yearned for Korean vegetables. The garden triggered memories of home for many older Korean immigrants, especially those with rural backgrounds.[91]

News of the light rail project devastated the gardeners. The rally to preserve the garden involved not only members of the Korean community but also neighborhood

Women working at the Korean Service Center, 2000; Grace Lee, founder, is in the front row, middle, and executive director Yunjoo Park is second from left in the back row

Somalis, who supported the Korean elders and were further concerned about the noise and other environmental issues. "It was an exemplary march of grassroots people power," recalls Park, who organized and led the march. As a result, the light rail transit line plan was redrawn, and the garden was kept for the Korean elders at its original location—a memorable victory for KSC and for the larger Korean community.

Today, KSC serves about fifty Korean elderly people with assisted living in a facility called the Grace Place. Numerous others use the center to access government-supported aid, meal delivery, and transportation. In addition to these social services, KSC also offers caregiver support programs and has organized workshops and

Korean Service Center rally to preserve the vegetable garden, 2000

classes to make people aware of community-related issues such as domestic violence and mental health. It operates a weekly Korean cuisine program called *Banchanbang*, selling small dishes of Korean food to its neighbors.

Embracing All Who Need a Place of Solace: Buddhist Temple Sam Bul Sa

Located in a quiet residential neighborhood in Andover, Buddhist temple Sam Bul Sa is a place of worship and meditation for almost fifty followers. The four-acre property was purchased in 2007; an existing home in which the head priestess resides and an additional temple serve the congregation for ceremonies and prayer meetings.

Sam Bul Sa was named after three Buddhist statues: the Buddha in the middle and two Buddhist saints (*Kwanseum bosal* and *Jijang bosal*) on each side. The temple, with Hyang Hee as the head priestess, was officially recognized by the Jogye Order of Korean Buddhism in 1990. But worshippers had already been gathering in Myongja Kim's home in Brooklyn Park for more than two years before the temple's founding. A devoted follower, Kim opened her own home and personally brought the statue of the Buddhist saint from Korea, purchasing an extra seat in the airplane for the statue itself. The number of followers swelled, and soon the living room became so full that people in the back could barely see the statue.

The Minnesota Association for Korean Americans (MAKA) was founded in 1995, initially as the Mothers Association for Korean Americans. Renamed in 2006, MAKA has played a crucial financial and social role in supporting Korean Americans in their pursuit of a college degree. The scholarship committee awards young Korean Americans, including Korean adoptees, to motivate their studies and instill a sense of pride about their heritage. Over the past twenty-three years, 315 students have benefitted from these scholarships. MAKA has also developed a social network connecting second-generation Korean students, adoptees, and their parents as one Korean American community.[x]

The three Buddhist statues inside Temple Sam Bul Sa

While the relocation in 2007 was a big celebration, the temple had been through difficult times. When Hyang Hee returned to Korea in 2012 after serving the congregation for more than twenty years, the temple was frequented by many visiting priests, but none served long term. "We have lost some regular followers over the past couple years, but we have been able to keep this place open and steady for anyone who wants to meditate or simply find a peaceful mind," says Chil Yong Kwon, who has witnessed the history of the temple since he came to Minnesota as a student at the University of Minnesota and joined the congregation in 1990. Kwon was also the headmaster of the Buddhist Korean language school (*Sunjae Hakkyo*) that started in 2003.

The arrival of current head priestess Noyeul in December 2017 brought more stability to the temple. "This temple was already well founded by the previous head priestess. I saw the potential of this temple and decided to serve, although my fellow priests in Korea tried to dissuade me from coming to Minnesota. It would be my first time in America, and they were mostly concerned about the unknown and the harsh winters of Minnesota. But I was confident that I could do it. If there are Koreans living in Minnesota, I can certainly live in Minnesota," says Noyeul, who shares her vision to expand the temple into a warm and welcoming place that can embrace all who want to rest and cherish peace.

From Invisible to Visible: Korean Adoptees in Minnesota

Minnesota is home to ten to fifteen thousand Korean adoptees. It is also the center of numerous Korean adoptee organizations and social networks. By the mid-1980s, the years with the highest numbers of Korean adoption, adoptive families and their Korean children sought to form a community. "What's kind of amazing is it seems like as Korean adoptees, we just kind of have this special unwritten bond with each other, that we just kind of know each other and what we've been through. It's kind of a special bond just having other friends that are Korean adoptees, as well, male and female," shares Susan March in an interview with the Minnesota Historical Society in 2011. Various Korean culture camps—including Korean Culture Camp of Minnesota (St. Paul), Kamp Kimchee (Brainerd), Camp Choson (St. Paul), and Camp Moon Hwa (Rochester)—and traditional Korean music and dance groups have become popular ways to learn and celebrate Korean traditions.

The first Korean culture camp started in 1976 at the Minnehaha Academy when the Korean Institute of Minnesota board members together with the parents of adopted children created a weeklong summer program for kindergarteners through sixth graders. The Korean Culture Camp of Minnesota (KCCM) program aimed to instill a sense of pride in the children and teach their Korean heritage—the culture, history, and customs of Korea. Activities included singing Korean children's songs, playing traditional Korean drums, and learning dances and taekwondo. By 1985 about three hundred children from California, Indiana, Texas, Ohio, and Minnesota attended the camp. In 1987 it became a Minnesota corporation, and in 1991 teachers were paid for the first time. The next year, when the daytime capacity of four hundred children was met, evening sessions accommodated more than one hundred additional campers. The mid-1990s were the peak years in which almost seven hundred children were enrolled (including children in nursery care) and more than a hundred were on a waiting list. Since 2000, the camp has maintained a steady number of two hundred fifty to three hundred campers with about two hundred adult volunteers and sixty teen helpers.[92]

In addition to KCCM, there are Camp Choson (established in 1993) and Kamp Kimchee (established in 1982), both designed to serve Korean adoptees but welcoming

Jang-mi Korean Dancers perform the Fan Dance for attendees of a camp for Korean children adopted by American families, Minnehaha Academy, Minneapolis, 1988.

anyone with Korean cultural tics and interests. Similarly, the Jang-mi Dance and Drum Group was created in 1984 to encourage Korean adoptees to learn about their heritage and find pride in their roots.[93]

Adult Korean adoptees, those who were adopted between the late 1960s and mid-1980s, established Minnesota Adopted Koreans in 1996 and Adopted Korean (AK) Connection in 2000. AK Connection provides a comprehensive website with up-to-date information and resources of interest to adult Korean adoptees in Minnesota. In addition, the organization hosts a variety of events and activities that foster friendship and networking and build a support system for Korean adoptees in the community.[94]

Another institution that specifically addresses this community is the Korean Adoptees Ministry Center (KAM). A faith-based nonprofit organization established in 2000, KAM focuses on the spiritual and religious aspect of adoptees' lives. KAM organizes annual Spiritual Journey trips to

Korean Adoptees Ministry Center Spiritual Journey trip, July 2012; Reverend Sung Chul Park at left

The Korean Adoptees Ministry Center was founded by Reverend Sung Chul Park, who moved to the United States in 1974 to pursue a master's degree in business administration at the University of Minnesota. He still remembers his surprise when he was introduced to his academic advisor's two Korean adoptee children. The meeting inspired concern about Korean adoptees' cultural connection to their homeland. While working several jobs after graduation, Reverend Park was also actively involved in the Korean Institute of Minnesota and Korean culture camps. He and his wife, Yunjoo Park (director of Korean Service Center), were particularly eager to meet and connect with local Korean adoptees. Yunjoo Park, at the time a Catholic Charities social worker, officially launched a group called Minnesota Adopted Koreans (MAK) in 1996: "MAK has seen its mailing list swell from four people at its beginning in the late 1980s to more than 300 in its 5th year as an official group." Members of MAK were instrumental in forming Adopted Korean (AK) Connection in 2000.[xi]

As the Parks interacted with more Korean adoptees, Reverend Park began to recognize the need for a spiritual and cultural ministry specific to them. He pursued a master's degree at McCormick Theological Seminary and was ordained as a minister upon graduation in 1998. Under Reverend Park's leadership and with the help of the local Korean Presbyterian Church of Minnesota and the Presbyterian Church USA denomination, the KAM Center was founded and sustained, celebrating its tenth anniversary in 2010.[xii]

provide opportunities for adult adoptees to visit their home country and explore their cultural roots.

Korean adoptees also receive attention from research specialists in Minnesota. The University of Minnesota is one of the leading institutions in transracial and transnational adoption research. Dr. Judith Eckerle, the director of the Adoption Medicine Clinic at the University of Minnesota and a Korean adoptee herself, offers specialized health care for internationally adopted children, focusing on their medical, developmental, cognitive, and mental health needs.[95]

Adoptive parents have also contributed to the Korean American community. For example, Martha Vickery and Stephen Wunrow, who adopted two children from Korea, have been a positive force for Korean adoptees in Minnesota, launching *Korean Quarterly* in 1997. Vickery and Wunrow realized how important it was to engage with the Korean American community and wanted their children

Martha Vickery and Stephen Wunrow family photo

to be aware of their cultural roots—to connect with other adoptees and their families and create a community of Korean Americans of all kinds. In an interview recorded for a documentary film on Korean adoptees in Minnesota, Wunrow shares a philosophy of parenting his two Korean adopted children: "Maybe sometimes we overdo it ... raising our kids and try to do all this Korean stuff ... we try to go to Korean church, go to Korean school, and take them to Korea ... some people say you are doing too much ... but our philosophy from the very beginning when they were really little was you can't do too much."[96]

Another publication bringing visibility to the Korean adoptee community is Kim Jackson and Heewon Lee's book, *Here: A Visual History of Adopted Koreans in Minnesota*. The book features a series of photographs that capture Korean adoptees as everyday people in Minnesota, recognizing them as a group that significantly shaped the state's immigration history.

Judo and Taekwondo in Minnesota

A group of dedicated judo instructors and students practiced at the state's first center, the Minnesota Judo Academy, by 1965. The academy was operated by Bong Soo Yang, formerly a head instructor for the Republic of Korea's army and a Korean Olympic team coach. He was invited to come to Minnesota by Insun Hong, who, also in 1965, started an employee judo club at 3M. Yang later moved to Chicago to run the Chicago Judo Center, but first he coached many Korean and non-Korean Minnesotans, sending talented students to Korea to train for state and national competitions.[97]

Hyon Jun Sun ("Jay") brought taekwondo to Minnesota, opening the first center in 1966. Before retiring in 1977, he operated six taekwondo schools, including the

In 1997, Martha Vickery and Stephen Wunrow founded *Korean Quarterly* (*KQ*), a newspaper that serves Minnesota's entire Korean American community. While attending the English Ministry (EM) of the Korean Presbyterian Church of Minnesota with their three children (two of them adopted from Korea), Vickery and Wunrow were inspired to create a newspaper that could bring the Korean community closer together.

Reverend "Sunny" Kang was working to connect with young Korean adoptees, organizing traditional events during the Korean holidays such as *Seolnal* and *Choosuk*. With Vickery and Wunrow, Kang helped create a small ministry of Outreach to Korean Adoptee Youth Group (OKAY) within the EM. Vickery and Wunrow saw that a newspaper that would serve as a voice for Korean adoptees and all Korean Americans in Minnesota presented an exciting opportunity. Vickery and Wunrow sent out letters to three thousand community members, including five hundred adoptive families, to describe their vision and invite subscriptions to the future publication. Surprisingly, close to one thousand subscriptions were paid even before the newspaper was officially out.

Today, *KQ* has a national and international circulation and covers issues of interest to the diverse Korean American community of first-generation immigrants and their children, adopted Koreans and their families, and other intercultural/interracial Korean American families. In addition, it attracts many non-Korean readers, including the parents and relatives of adopted Koreans and other Asian Americans. *KQ* appeals to people who are interested in Korean culture and history, the Korean American community, or racial and ethnic identity issues of minority populations in America. *KQ* has received more than twenty-five awards of excellence, including from the Minnesota Newspaper Association, the Independent Press Association, and Community Service Awards from the president of Korea and the Korean Association of Minnesota. *Korean Quarterly* is a member of the Korean American Journalists Association.[xiii]

The cover of the fall 2017 issue of *Korean Quarterly* features *Arirang*: a Korean traditional performing arts concert. Three Twin Cities performing groups—Shinparam Korean drumming troupe, Minnesota Korean Women's Choir, and the Jang-mi Dance and Drum—came together for a collaborative performance.

Shinparam (Korean for exhilaration or enthusiasm) is a traditional Korean percussion music (Samulnori) group formed in 2004. Sarah Lee, a second-generation Korean American, together with Stephen Wunrow and Martha Vickery of *Korean Quarterly*, organized this new group consisting of one-and-a-half- and second-generation Korean Americans—including the Wunrow kids—who had taken an interest in playing. The group first performed in St. Benedict, Minnesota.

Over time, more people joined their weekly practice, and in 2005, Kim Duk Soo, a famous Korean Samulnori performer and the inspiration for forming Shinparam, invited them to participate in the international Samulnori Festival in Buyeo. Shinparam has been a regular fixture at many Korean-related events in the community, including the Lunar New Year celebration at the Korean Service Center, the Korean American Association's annual picnic, and even fund-raising events for the Sejong Academy in St. Paul. The group also performs annually at the Chicago Korean Festival and occasionally trains in Korea at the Hanullim school of music in Buyeo. According to Martha and Stephen, "Samulnori allows you to experience the Korean culture that speaks through your mind and emotions . . . it is a music that heals and encourages."[xiv]

Shinparam performance at the Korean Service Center's Lunar New Year's celebration, 2006

Insun Hong, 1965. Noted for being the first Korean employee at 3M, Insun Hong was also the first to introduce judo to the Twin Cities. He was already a fifth *dan* holder in heavy weight when he started the 3M judo club in 1965. While some were skeptical about the level of interest in judo, more than two hundred employees showed up on the first day. Hong also served as chief instructor of judo at the Maplewood Junior High School. At the same time, as the owner of two judo centers in the Twin Cities, he continued to sponsor the immigration of instructors. In 1968, he also became the chief coordinator for the Pan American trials tournament.

Bloomington Karate Center that opened in 1974 at the corner of Ninety-eighth Street and Lyndale Avenue. In 1973, Moon Kim came from Korea, taught in Minneapolis and Bloomington, and opened a taekwondo center in St. Paul, which was the facility that put taekwondo on the local map. Under master instructor Kim, the first Amateur Athletic Union–sanctioned taekwondo tournament was staged at the University of Minnesota's Williams Arena in May 1979. The crowd was small, but the publicity brought positive results. By 1982, the Minnesota Taekwondo Association reported that more than five thousand Americans had learned the skills since the sport was introduced to Minnesota in 1965.[98]

Taekwondo first appeared as a demonstration sport at the opening ceremony of the 1988 Summer Olympic games in South Korea. Ever since, it has had a national profile as a unique martial art, becoming an official Olympic medal sport in 2000. Today, numerous taekwondo centers across the state promote the art of Korean-style self-defense.

The Future of the Korean Community

The Challenges of Cultivating Support and Involvement

"When I first immigrated in 1975, I feel like the Koreans were respected and we walked proudly. After 40 years, it looks like our children have good jobs, but they don't seem much interested in the Korean community. I feel like our generation is partly responsible for that," writes Hyun Sook Han, president of the Korean American Association of Minnesota (KAAM). "It's not just the amount of donations, but the amount of 'passion in participating' that drives the Korean American Association."[99]

Sejong Academy in St. Paul is Minnesota's first Korean immersion school. It opened in 2014 in response to parents seeking to ensure that children were in touch with their heritage. Seven years of planning went into creating it. Executive director Brad Tipka says, "I believe that Korea as a country and Korean as a language represent strong opportunities for students in Minnesota. . . . What I saw in Korea and what stands out for me about Korean people is a dedication to family, education, hard work, and persistence—these are all great qualities to instill in our students." Tipka lived and taught in Busan and Seoul, Korea, for five years, developing a strong love for the language and the culture.

Sejong Academy opened with sixty-three students from kindergarten to sixth grade but expanded to prekindergarten through eighth grade. The academy initially aimed to serve Korean adoptees, but a

Sejong Academy paper tiger craft

significant number of Karen immigrant children from Myanmar, part of a large community in St. Paul, also enrolled, and now the school offers Karen language courses as well. Sejong Academy's Korean immersion curriculum includes not only enhanced Korean language classes but also cultural extracurricular activities, such as advanced taekwondo, Korean dance, and traditional Korean theater.[xv]

One challenge the Korean community faces is involving the younger generation in celebrating its heritage. The community was built out of a strongly felt necessity by first-generation immigrants who couldn't find much Korean-ness in Minnesota other than themselves; members of the US–born generations are surrounded by a more diverse population with many more Korean resources available to them. The need to get involved in sustaining and expanding the community has become less relevant to many new immigrants and their children.

When KAAM was on the verge of being dissolved due to lack of participation in 1976, board member Stephan Huh called for reestablishing the organization's identity to focus on governmental activities that connect with American society and to launch projects that allow the younger Korean generation to maintain their connections to and pride in their ancestral home. Reinventing its purpose helped KAAM continue to thrive in times of limited enthusiasm.[100]

Its newest project, KAAM VOICE (Voter Organizing Initiative and Community Empowerment), started in 2018 to advocate for the community in Minnesota by helping Koreans register to vote, campaigning for increasing voter turnout, operating a citizenship class to teach potential applicants about the process of naturalization, and also fighting for the rights of Korean adoptees in the United States, especially those facing deportation because their adoptive parents did not apply for their citizenship. KAAM also joined the Korean American Grassroots Conference, a nationwide network of Korean American voters. As KAAM adds initiatives that connect the local Korean community to the larger Korean American civil society, it continues to strengthen its position representing Korean Americans in Minnesota.

However, some still believe that the overall role of the Korean community will gradually become less relevant, and

Mehee Coolidge and her husband, David Coolidge, on election day, November 6, 2018

eventually Koreans will culturally assimilate, just as have many early immigrants of various European states who are now almost indistinguishable within the US population. While the current Korean community in Minnesota consists of mainly Korea-born first-generation immigrants, they are also aging. According to US Census data, in 2016, there were about 245 more Koreans over the age of sixty-five and 4,410 more Koreans between the ages of eighteen and sixty-five than in 2000. The number of Koreans through age seventeen shrank by about 2,892 in that span. Even though Koreans will continue to migrate to Minnesota, their population will probably not exceed the surge of the 1970s.

The gradually reducing number of second-generation Koreans in the state and the limited arrivals of new immigrants may weaken the ties and the commitment of Koreans to the Korean community. Unless Koreans continue to develop a strong sense of cultural pride and educate their children in their ancestral heritage, the fate of a distinct and prominent community may be at stake.

The Challenges of Becoming Fully Inclusive

As the Korean student population connected to the University of Minnesota and other colleges continues to grow, the number of graduates settling in Minnesota for jobs and further opportunities will increase as well. A constant influx of Koreans moving to Minnesota from other states diversifies the migration experiences of Koreans in the state. Interracially married Koreans and their children as well as Korean adoptees and their families add more ethnic variety to what was once a fairly monolithic group. Differences in political and social perspectives among the generations only highlight shifting dynamics in the Korean community.

Despite the changing demographics, ingrained prejudice can make interculturally married Koreans feel isolated from Minnesota's Korean community. Also, some Korean adoptees have felt rejected by Korean immigrants who view the adoptees as not culturally Korean enough. Such views will change and likely diminish as younger Koreans display greater acceptance of racial and cultural difference than did members of their parents' generation. Recent immigrants from Korea tend to be more politically and socially liberal, having been exposed to the changes of what used to be a rather homogeneous and conservative nation. Change is inevitable; the Korean community will have to adapt to its shifting population but also continue to serve all Korean Americans and celebrate its distinctive Korean identity.

"It is time for us to once again get together and strive for a larger community and voice [for] ourselves so we can pass on a better future to our descendants.... I hope that all forms of gatherings will make the Korean society more vibrant so it can be a part of the mainstream society here in Minnesota," writes Hyun Sook Han in the 2018 KAAM newsletter as she retired from her position as president. KAAM's new president, Mehee Coolidge, draws on experience from her work at the Korean American Women's Association and hopes to bring more interest and enthusiasm to the Korean community.[101]

For more than sixty years, Koreans have been part of Minnesota's ethnic history. Today and into the future, they continue to contribute to the vibrancy of America's colorful cultural mosaic.

Personal Account: Soon Ja Lee

Soon Ja Lee is the wife of Yun Ho Lee, referred to by many as the founding father of the Minnesota Korean community. The Lees were deeply involved in supporting numerous organizations, institutions, and events that helped local Koreans become more connected to and supportive of each other. The following account is excerpted and edited from Soon Ja Lee's 2012 memoir, *My Husband, Yun Ho Lee,* mainly focusing on the early story of her efforts to support his studies and their business. Yun Ho Lee died in 2009 at the age of ninety-one.

When we married in 1948, I was a sophomore in vocal performance at the Seoul National University. My husband even as a child always dreamt of studying in the United States. In 1949, with full scholarship from the University of Jamestown in North Dakota [previously known as Jamestown College], my husband and I crossed the Pacific Ocean to come to the United States. While my husband was majoring in accounting, I was able to take a few classes in vocal performance as a part-time student. Even though my husband was on a scholarship, there were additional expenses that made it inevitable for us to both work in the university cafeteria. My husband earned seventy-five cents an hour, whereas I made only forty-five cents because I was a woman. During the summer break, my husband worked at a nearby creamery as a butter wrapper making $1.25 per hour.

While working full time during the summer and working part time at the cafeteria during the semester, my husband always made the dean's list. He always studied late into the night; even the university security person said that the light in our student apartment was always on until daybreak. I remember, one time, how my husband suffered from pneumonia and we had to spend all of our money on paying for the medicine. We didn't know back then that students didn't need to pay for medical treatment.

After all the hardship of studying and working part-time jobs, my husband finally completed his undergraduate studies in 1953 and enrolled in the accounting master's program at the University of Minnesota. Initially, I continued to take classes in vocal performance and piano, but it became extremely difficult for us to financially support both our studies. Since my husband's schedule made it impossible for him to work during the semester, I decided to work full time at a sewing factory. As I started to work and sometimes was unable to cook meals, my husband had to eat instant ramen noodles.

Finally, my husband graduated in 1955, and got a job at Cargill. We were able to move out of the student apartment, and for the first time became homeowners of a small two-bedroom, two-stories house not too far from the University Avenue in Minneapolis.

Around this time, faculty from the Seoul National University began to arrive in the Twin Cities. They came as part of a sisterhood contract with the University of Minnesota and were mostly by themselves, having left their families in Korea. So on weekends, we went fishing with them and cooked what we caught (mostly sunfish) at our house since there was no worries about the smell. Sometimes we made spicy soup; sometimes we fried them on a skillet.

After three years at Cargill, my husband worked for another four years at the International Multifoods Corporation, and with our savings we were able to pilot start a small in-home sewing business with just four sewing machines in the basement in 1962. In 1965, we officially registered the business and received a business permit under the name of Lee's Apron Manufacturing Company. We were able to obtain business contracts from Woolworth, Kmart, Target, Grant, and even the military. During this process of expansion, we moved our factory several times to more spacious places and opened a second factory in Rush City, north of Minneapolis. We always hired about four to five Koreans, mostly wives of students at the University of Minnesota who were skilled in sewing. I was in charge of fixing and maintaining various sewing machines. I

Yun Ho Lee and
Soon Ja Lee

was already trained by the technicians in how to fix the machines when they installed them, so my role as the "utility man" was saving us a lot of money.

I was always accompanying my husband when he had to drive out of town to look out for new market opportunities. I was doing as much sewing work as possible in the car. One cold day, our car spun out [on] the frozen road and hit the guardrail. The engine broke and we were stuck in the car in the freezing cold for several hours waiting for help to arrive.

As we started to make some money through our endless efforts and the business that we built from the ground up, my husband and I decided to donate funds to Jamestown College and the University of Minnesota to pay our gratitude. My husband didn't stop there. He was actively involved in the Korean American Association, serving as the president multiple times and organizing important events such as the Aquatennial. Being part of the Aquatennial in 1970 was a major honor to the Korean society, and it was my husband's effort [to] ask for the full support of the Korean community that led the Korean Americans in Minnesota to participate in this major event.

In 1990, when the Korean Service Center opened, we were so moved by the effort of Grace Lee, who was voluntarily helping the Korean elderly without any monetary compensation. So my husband not only asked the Koreans to support the organization, but became a major financial contributor.

We were also the early members of the Korean bible study. First formed by a few Korean faculty at the University of Minnesota, the bible study group grew into a Korean Christian fellowship that eventually became the Minnesota First Korean Church. My husband became the elder of this church. At that time, most Koreans were either newcomers or students, so as an early settler and business owner, we always felt the responsibility to assist the church in any way we could.

There were always a lot of Koreans visiting our home. Especially, there were many Korean students studying at the University of Minnesota, and exchange faculty members from the Seoul National University. I frequently invited people to our house for Korean meals and my husband was practically the chauffer, bringing them in and driving them back. Many of them became influential people upon their return to Korea. When we visited Korea thirty-six years [after] we left, some of the University of Minnesota graduates we knew who returned to Korea hosted a banquet to welcome our visit.

We didn't have any children, but we loved and cherished each other as if it would be for our children. Despite his lymphoma diagnosis and the chemotherapy, nor the aspiration pneumonia, which left him in the hospital for several months, [nothing] stopped him from helping the people around him and my relatives. His last moments were of happiness and satisfaction of seeing our relatives and people we know in content.

For Further Reading

Ch'oe, Yŏng-ho. *From the Land of Hibiscus: Koreans in Hawai'i, 1903–1950.* Honolulu: University of Hawai'i Press, 2007.

Flanigan, James. *The Korean-American Dream: Portraits of a Successful Immigrant Community.* Reno: University of Nevada Press, 2018.

Holmquist, June Drenning. *They Chose Minnesota: A Survey of the State's Ethnic Groups.* St. Paul: Minnesota Historical Society Press, 1988.

Hurh, Won Moo. *The Korean Americans.* The New Americans. Westport, CT: Greenwood Press, 1998.

Kim, Eleana Jean. *Adopted Territory: Transnational Korean Adoptees and the Politics of Belonging.* Durham, NC: Duke University Press, 2010.

Kim, Hyung-chan. *The Korean Diaspora: Historical and Sociological Studies of Korean Immigration and Assimilation in North America.* Santa Barbara, CA: ABC-Clio, 1977.

Kim, Ilpyong J. *Korean-Americans: Past, Present, and Future.* Elizabeth, NJ: Hollym International, 2004.

Min, Pyong Gap. *Koreans in North America: Their Twenty-First Century Experiences.* Lanham, MD: Lexington Books, 2013.

Park Nelson, Kim. *Invisible Asians: Korean American Adoptees, Asian American Experiences, and Racial Exceptionalism.* Asian American Studies Today. New Brunswick, NJ: Rutgers University Press, 2016.

Patterson, Wayne. *The Ilse: First-Generation Korean Immigrants in Hawai'i, 1903–1973.* Hawai'i Studies on Korea. Honolulu: University of Hawai'i Press, 2000.

Patterson, Wayne. *The Korean Frontier in America: Immigration to Hawaii, 1896–1910.* Honolulu: University of Hawai'i Press, 1988.

Patterson, Wayne, and Hyung-chan Kim. *The Koreans in America.* In America. Minneapolis: Lerner Publications, 1977.

Tuan, Mia, and Jiannbin Lee Shiao. *Choosing Ethnicity, Negotiating Race: Korean Adoptees in America.* New York: Russell Sage Foundation, 2011.

Notes

Oral history interviews that contributed to this narrative:

Asians in Minnesota Oral History Project (1979–80), Minnesota Historical Society, St. Paul (interviews by Sarah Mason):

Philip Ahn, Mary Kim Bilek, Hyun Sook Han, Yung Lyun Ko, Sang H. Lee, Sung Won Son, Joo Ho Sung

Korean Community Oral History Project (1994, 2011), Minnesota Historical Society, St. Paul (interviews by Sophia Kim and Insung Oh):

John Choi, JinHee Darmer, Sarah Imm, Jong Bum Kwon, Susan March

Minnesota Ethnic History Project Reords (1969–80), Minnesota Historical Society, St. Paul (interviews by Sarah Mason):

Philip Ahn, Reverend Seo Young Baik, Reverend Francis Choe, Neal Gault, Hak Rhim Han, Ki Yong Kim, Young Shil Song, Joo Ho Sung

Interviewed by the author (2017–18):

Yeon Joo Cho (Lucia Kim), Insun Hong, Stephan Huh, Nicole Johnson, Kyeonghe Kim, Sang H. Kim, Tae Hwan Kim, Chil Yong Kwon and Noyeul Priestess (Sambulsa), Changjae Lee, Brooke Newmaster, Sung Chul Park, Yunjoo Park, Hak Cheol Shin, Chang Won Song , Stephen Wunrow and Martha Vickery, Changseung Yoo

1. "The Asian Population," *2010 Census Briefs* (US Census Bureau, March 2012); Jie Zong and Jeanne Batalova, "Korean Immigrants in the United States," *Migration Information Source*, February 8, 2017, migrationpolicy.org; American Community Survey (US Census Bureau, 2016).

2. Duk Hee Lee Murabayashi, "Korean Passengers Arriving at Honolulu, 1903–1905" (Center for Korean Studies, School of Hawaiian, Asian and Pacific Studies, University of Hawaii at Manoa, 2001), 7–8.

3. "A Large Party Come by the Gaelic: One Hundred and Two Subjects of the Hermit Kingdom Reach Here to Try Their Luck at Plantation Labor," *The Hawaiian Star*, January 3, 1903, 1; Wayne Patterson, *The Korean Frontier in America: Immigration to Hawaii, 1896–1910* (Honolulu: University of Hawaii Press, 1988).

4. Hyekyeung Hyun, "The Jeju Workers Who Immigrated to Hawaii," *Jeju Shinbo*, December 30, 2018; Patterson, *The Korean Frontier in America*, 25–27.

5. Sarah Mason, "The Koreans," in *They Chose Minnesota: A Survey of the State's Ethnic Groups,* ed. June Drenning Holmquist (St. Paul: Minnesota Historical Society Press, 1981); Wayne Patterson, "Sugar-Coated Diplomacy: Horace Allen and Korean Immigration to Hawaii, 1902–1905," *Diplomatic History* 3, no. 1 (1979): 19–38; Lee Houchins and Chang-Su Houchins, "The Korean Experience in America, 1903–1924," in *The Asian American: The Historical Experience*, ed. Norris Hundley, Jr. (Santa Barbara, CA: ABC-Clio, 1976), 130–36; Hyung-Chan Kim and Wayne Patterson, *The Koreans in America,* In America Series (Minneapolis: Lerner Publishing Group, 1993); Fred Harrington, *God, Mammon, and the Japanese: Dr. Horace N. Allen and*

Korean-American Relations, 1884–1905 (Madison: University of Wisconsin Press, 1944), 186; "The Koreans in Hawaii," *Korea Review* (November 1906): 401–6, in Duk Hee Lee Murabayashi, "How Koreans Were Viewed in Hawaii: 1903–1906."

6. Mason, "The Koreans"; Houchins and Houchins, "The Korean Experience," 129; Warren Kim, *Koreans in America* (Seoul: Po Chin Chai Printing Co., 1971), 28–31; Kingsley Lyu, "Korean Nationalist Activities in Hawaii and the Continental United States, 1900–1919," *Amerasia Journal* 4 (1977): 31–33; Yong-ho Choe, "A Brief History of Christ United Methodist Church, 1903–2003," in *Christ United Methodist Church, 1903–2003: A Pictorial History* (Honolulu: Christ Methodist Church, 2003).

7. Wayne Patterson, *The Ilse: First-Generation Korean Immigrants in Hawai'i, 1903–1973,* Hawai'i Studies on Korea (Honolulu: University of Hawai'i Press and Center for Korean Studies, 2000).

8. Pyong Gap Min, "Koreans' Immigration to the US: History and Contemporary Trends," Research Report 3 (Research Center for Korean Community, Queens College, CUNY, January 27, 2011), 3; Bong-Youn Choy, *Koreans in America* (Chicago: Nelson-Hall, 1979), 143.

9. Choy, *Koreans in America*, 88–89.

10. Alice Yun Chai, "Feminist Analysis of Life Histories of Hawaii's Early Asian Immigrant Women," *Asian Journal of Women's Studies* 2 (October 31, 1996): 5.

11. Paul Choi and Hanjung Lee, "The Korean Independence Movement and Boston University" (Center for Global Christianity and Mission, Boston University School of Theology).

12. Kim, *Koreans in America*, 23–26, 36, 53, 91–98; Houchins and Houchins,

"The Korean Experience," 139, 156; Howard Melendy, *Asians in America: Filipinos, Koreans, and East Indians* (Woodbridge, CT: Twayne Publishers, 1977), 129–30, 137; Pyong Gap Min, "The Korean Community in the United States: Changes in the Twenty-First Century" (paper, International Conference on Korean Diaspora Studies, September 28, 2013), 5; New England Centennial Committee of Korean Immigration to the United States, *History of Koreans in New England* (Seoul: Seon-Hak Publishing, 2004).

13. Ji-Hye Shin, "Unresolved Military Conflict Between North and South Korea That Drew the United States and Communist China into the Fighting," immigrationtounitedstates.org.

14. Among Minnesotans, 94,646 have served; 948 were killed in action, 154 were listed as missing in action, and 1,500 were wounded. Korean War Memorial, St. Paul, MN.

15. Bok-lim Kim, "Asian Wives of US Servicemen: Women in Shadows," *Amerasia Journal* 4, no. 1 (1977): 98; Won Moo Hurh and Kwang Chung Kim, *Korean Immigrants in America: A Structural Analysis of Ethnic Confinement and Adhesive Adaptation* (Cranbury, NJ: Fairleigh Dickinson University Press, 1984), 49.

16. Arissa Oh, *To Save the Children of Korea: The Cold War Origins of International Adoption* (Palo Alto, CA: Stanford University Press, 2015); Jae Ran Kim, "Korean Adoption in Minnesota," in *HERE: A Visual History of Adopted Koreans in Minnesota,* ed. Kim Jackson and Heewon Lee (St. Paul, MN: Yeong & Yeong Book Company, 2010), 21; Bertha Holt, *The Seed from the East* (Los Angeles: Oxford Press, 1956); "The Legacy of Bertha 'Grandma' Holt," holtinternational.org.

17. National Association of Korean Americans, "In Observance of Centennial of Korean Immigration to the US," ed. John H. Kim, with Ji-Yeon Yuh, Elaine Kim, and Eui-Young Yu, 2003, naka.org; Eleana Kim, "Korean Adoptees' Role in the United States," in *Korean-Americans: Past, Present, and Future,* ed. Ilpyong J. Kim (Carlsbad, CA: Hollym International Corporation, 2004), 181; Hurh and Kim, *Korean Immigrants in America,* 49; Kim Park Nelson, "Korean Transracial Adoption in Minnesota," *MNopedia,* Minnesota Historical Society.

18. Kim, *Koreans in America,* 26; Min, "Koreans' Immigration to the US."

19. Hyun Sook Kim and Pyong Gap Min, "The Post-1965 Korean Immigrants: Their Characteristics and Settlement Patterns," *Korea Journal of Population and Development* 21, no. 2 (December 1992): 132–35; In-Jin Yoon, "A Cohort Analysis of Korean Immigrants' Class Backgrounds and Socioeconomic Status in the United States," *Korea Journal of Population and Development* 26, no. 1 (July 1997): 67.

20. Jong Hak Hong, "The History of the Koreatown in New York and New Jersey," *Korea Times,* January 2, 2019; National Association of Korean Americans, "In Observance of Centennial."

21. Ui Seon Kang, "Changes in South Korean Emigration: Focusing on Emigration to North America," master's thesis, Graduate School of International Studies, Seoul National University, 2015; Yoon, "A Cohort Analysis," 67.

22. Kim and Min, "The Post-1965 Korean Immigrants," 126.

23. "Statistical Yearbook," Immigration and Naturalization Services (1979–2001); Pyong Gap Min, "The Immigration of Koreans to the United States: A Review of Forty-Five Year (1965–2009) Trends," in *Koreans in North America: Their Twenty-First Century Experiences,* ed. Pyong Gap Min (New York: Lexington Books, 2013), 10.

24. Yoon, "A Cohort Analysis," 65.

25. "Statistical Yearbook," Immigration and Naturalization Services (1979–2001); Min, "Koreans' Immigration to the US," 9, 12–13, 20–21.

26. Mason, "The Koreans," 571; US Department of Justice, Immigration and Naturalization Services, Annual Reports; Eui-young Yu, "Koreans in America: An Emerging Ethnic Minority," *Amerasia Journal* 4, no. 1 (1977): 117–23; "Hmong and Koreans are Minnesota's Largest Asian Groups" (Minnesota Planning, news release), October 9, 1991, and "Prosperity Realized by Many Koreans," *Star Tribune,* April 18, 1993, 20A—both box 2, folder 17, series 8: newspaper clippings, subseries 1: Southeast Asia, Minnesota Population 1990, Immigration History Research Center and Archives, University of Minnesota, Minneapolis (hereafter, IHRC).

27. According to Migration Policy Institute, the term *immigrant* (or *foreign born*) refers to people residing in the United States who were not US citizens at birth. This population includes, naturalized citizens, lawful permanent residents, certain legal nonimmigrants (e.g., persons on student or work visas), those admitted under refugee or asylum status, and persons illegally residing in the United States. US Census Bureau, 2011–15 American Community Survey, Minority and Citizenship Status in the US, Minnesota, Koreans Alone. According to the Comparative Demographic Estimates, 2012–16 American Community Survey 5-Year Estimates, among Asians, Minnesota has the largest percentage of Hmong

people (2.2 percent); Asian Indians are second (0.7 percent); and Chinese and Vietnamese are the third-largest group of Asians (0.5 percent) in Minnesota.

28. Mason, "The Koreans," 573; Department of Commerce and Labor, US Bureau of Labor Statistics, *Bulletin of the Bureau of Labor* 84 (Washington, DC: Government Printing Office, 1909), 345, 348, 349.

29. Mason, "The Koreans," 573; *Hamline Oracle*, October 6, 1925, 1, Archives Digital Collections, Hamline University; *St. Paul Pioneer Press*, February 1, 1925, 8; "Chang Yun Called to Korean Home by Starvation in Family," *Hamline Oracle*, October 16, 1925, 4, Archives Digital Collections, Hamline University.

30. "Cosmopolitan Campus," *Weekly Mac*, October 3, 1952, 3, College Archives Digital Collections, Macalester College. There were sixty-one students from twenty-nine countries enrolled at Macalester in 1952. Macalester ranked in the top ten percent in comparative enrollment of foreign students among small private colleges.

31. Mason, "The Koreans," 574; *Weekly Mac*, February 11, 1949, 3, and "Korean Student Arrives Here," *Mac Weekly*, July 14, 1950, 3—both College Archives Digital Collections, Macalester College.

32. Soon Ja Lee, *My Husband, Yun Ho Lee* (Seoul: Yesol Press, 2012). Insun Hong came to Minnesota in 1962, entered 3M in 1964, and retired in 2000. He was vice president of the Superabrasives and Microfinishing Systems Division, which he built while at 3M.

33. J. L. Morrill, "The President's Page," *The Minnesotan: The University Staff Magazine* (December 1954): 15, and "How the U Helped Seoul University Rebuild

after the Ravages of War," *The Minnesotan* (December 1956): 3–7—both in Arthur E. Schneider papers, SNU of Korea folder, information files, University Archives, University of Minnesota (hereafter, Schneider papers); Young Mok Chung, *The University of Minnesota Project*, 146.

34. Tae Choon Kim, "Remembering Elder Yun Ho Lee," in Lee, *My Husband, Yun Ho Lee*, 129–30.

35. Ock-Joo Kim and Hwang Sang-Ik, "Minnesota Project: The Influence of American Medicine on the Development of Medical Education and Medical Research in Post-War Korea," *Korean Journal of Medical History* 9 (June 2000): 112–23, Schneider papers; Jiyun Lee, "Do You Know the Minnesota Project?" *Hankuk Kyongjae*, September 15, 2015; Miyoung Kim, "Minnesota Project: I Open the Heart with a Trembling Hand," March 2, 2009.

36. Mason, "The Koreans," 575.

37. Mason, "The Koreans," 575.

38. Koreans in Minnesota—TC, Servicemen's Wives, box 20, MEHP; *Korean Elder Association Newsletter*, seventh anniversary special edition (1985). Almost no public data on domestic violence issues against Korean women married to American men exists, but anecdotal evidence via personal interviews has uncovered several tragic incidents involving violence and abuse. Part of the problem was that many returning servicemen had a hard time finding steady jobs or were having alcohol problems. One incident in the late 1970s involved a Korean woman (Ok Soon Lee) killing her husband and herself after being constantly abused, alarming the Korean community regarding these women's struggles. Mason, "The Koreans," 575: attorneys were Theodore G.

Elmquist, also the husband of Young Shil Song, and Joseph Kaminsky.

39. *The Kernel: A Korean Community Newsletter in Minnesota*, January 1, 1971, 7, Korean American Association of Minnesota archives, St. Paul (hereafter, KAAM).

40. Mason, "The Koreans," 575; Korean Businesses in Minnesota—Twin Cities folder, box 20, MEHP.

41. "Makenna Dawson," 2014, Immigrant Stories Collection, Immigration History Research Center and Archives, Minneapolis, MN (hereafter, IHRC).

42. "Suzanne Johnson," January 31, 2017, Immigrant Stories Collection, IHRC.

43. *Minnesota Arirang (Part 2),* directed by Il Mook Hwang, May 2017, Jeon Joo MBC, Jeon Joo, Korea.

44. Kaomi Goetz, "Minnesota Adoptees Forge Bonds, Find Kinship in South Korea Visit," MPR News, August 18, 2016.

45. *Minnesota Arirang (Part 2).*

46. Nikolas Nadeau, "From One Korean Minnesotan to Another: Welcome Byung Ho Park," *Star Tribune*, December 18, 2015.

47. It is difficult to obtain an accurate estimate of the Korean adoptee population. According to the 2011–15 American Community Survey of the US Census, among the 16,034 Koreans (single race), 948 are estimated to be adoptees, indicating their status as "US citizen, born abroad of American parents." "Orphan Trains: Placing Out Children in Minnesota: Overview," LibGuides, Gale Family Library, Minnesota History Center.

48. Kim Park Nelson, *Invisible Asians: Korean American Adoptees, Asian American Experiences, and Racial Exceptionalism* (New Brunswick, NJ: Rutgers University Press, 2016), 101–2; Nelson, "Korean Transracial Adoption in Minnesota."

49. Mason, "The Koreans," 575; Tammy Ko Robinson and Becky Belcore, "Korean Adoptees Share Koreanness: A Parenthesis of History," in *Koreans in the Windy City: 100 Years of Korean Americans in the Chicago Area*, ed. Hyock Chun (New Haven, CT: East Rock Institute, 2005), 231; "Adoptions/Few Korean Children," *Star Tribune*, January 29, 1992, 1B, New Life in US, series 8, newspaper clippings, subseries 1: Southeast Asia, IHRC.

50. Goetz, "Minnesota Adoptees Forge Bonds"; "Why Adoptions Are So Rare in South Korea," *The Economist*, May 27, 2015.

51. Mason, "The Koreans," 577; Sung Soo Kim, "1975–1980: The Pride of Minnesota Koreans," *Korean Elderly Society Newsletter*, seventh anniversary edition (1985): 133.

52. Woojin Byun, "A Brief History of Korean Lawyers Trained in Minnesota," typed notes, October 2012, KAAM.

53. Aaron Kahn, "Dr. Sung Won Son, An Economist Who Can Talk to the 'Average Guy,'" *St. Paul Pioneer Press*, December 18, 1980, 2F, box 20, MEHP.

54. Many residents of the east side suburbs of Woodbury and Stillwater are employees of the 3M company. Siyoung Park, "The Residential Mobility of Koreans in Minneapolis–St. Paul," unpublished manuscript, 6–8, KAAM.

55. Mason, "The Koreans," 577.

56. Park, "Residential Mobility," 6–8.

57. K. Connie Kang, "Korean Churches Growing Rapidly," *Los Angeles Times*, November 1, 2008; Won Moo Hurh, *The Korean Americans,* The New Americans (Westport, CT: Greenwood Press, 1998).

58. *Annual Statistical Report of International Students and Scholars* (University of Minnesota, 2016–17).

59. The 2000 US Census data and the

Decennial Census and American Community Survey of 2012–16 do not specifically offer a Korean adoptee category. The Korean adoptee population is included in the data category as either "US citizen, born abroad of American parents" or "Foreign-born children with native-born parents."

60. "Groups at a Glance: Korean-Foreign Born Population, Minnesota 2000–2016," Minnesota Compass.

61. Choy, *Koreans in America*, 224–25.

62. Hurh, *The Korean Americans*, 106; Hyung-Chan Kim and Wayne Patterson, *The Koreans in America, 1882–1974* (Dobbs Ferry, NY: Oceana, 1974), 127; Choy, *Koreans in America*, 256–57.

63. Pastor Kim of KFBC resigned two months after the church was formed. The next two pastors were Kang Ho Lee and Chae Sub Shim.

64. A year later, in 1980, Pastor Baik left for Columbus, Ohio. Succeeding pastors include Choon Shik Lee from Korea and Reverend Yeo Sang Cho.

65. Lori Sturdevant, "Closer Ties Between Korean Congregation, HAUMC is Dr. Kim's Aim," *Century 2: Hennepin Avenue United Methodist Church's Newsletter*, October 28, 1980, 2, archival material shared by Tae Hwan Kim.

66. Personal notes from Chong Hae Chung, shared by Ji Suk Chung (Chong Hae Chung played a critical part in negotiating the unification of the two Presbyterian churches).

67. *Minnesota Korean Newsletter* 6, no. 5 (1979): 3, Koreans in Minnesota—TC, Kim Sung Soo, box 20, MEHP.

68. Elder Woo Bum Lee, "Watching the Process of Unification," *Dolbegae* (the Architect), ten-year anniversary special edition, Korean Presbyterian Church of Minnesota, 340–44.

69. Church of All Nations, Columbia Heights, MN, website.

70. Seventh-day Adventist Minneapolis Korean Church website; notes by unknown author, 1986, KAAM.

71. Notes by unknown author, 1986, KAAM.

72. "The Catholic Church of the Korean Community," *Joo Bo* (weekly newsletter), April 25 and May 2, 1982.

73. "The Catholic Church of the Korean Community," *Joo Bo*, May 4 and 16, 1982; "Korean Catholics Plagued by Vandals," *St. Paul Pioneer/St. Paul Dispatch*, May 2, 1981, box 22, MEHP.

74. Mason, "The Koreans," 575–76; *Korean Elderly Society Newsletter*, seventh anniversary edition (1985): 111–13; Aquatennial "Seas of the Orient," Minneapolis: July 17–26, 1970, Koreans in MN—TC, Aquatennial, box 20, MEHP.

75. Shin Heng Huh, "Me and the Korean American Association of Minnesota," *Korean Elderly Society Newsletter*, seventh anniversary edition (1985): 121–30.

76. Huh, "Me and the Korean American Association of Minnesota."

77. Proclamation of Korean Day by Governor Rudy Perpich, October 3, 1978, KAAM.

78. Notes on events and activities, KAAM.

79. Notes on events and activities, KAAM; "Minnesota Zoo to Provide Olympic Mascots," *Nashua Telegraph*, April 1, 1986, 17.

80. *Korean American Association of Minnesota Newsletter* 2 (2016): 1.

81. Yung Lyun Ko was the first presi-

dent of KIM. His academic background as an assistant professor in education at Konkuk University played a crucial role in developing the curriculum. Tae Hwan Kim, written notes, KAAM.

82. Denise Kotula, "Program Helps Korean Adoptees Adjust," *Minnesota Daily*, May 12, 1978, 8, 20.

83. Korean Institute of Minnesota website.

84. Bomi Yoon, Principal and Executive Director of KIM, correspondence with the author, August 10, 2018.

85. Gunryul Kim, "Mission Statement," February 25, 1978, *Korean Elderly Society Newsletter*, seventh anniversary edition (1985).

86. "Interview with Eun Woo Lee, Chairman of the Korean Elder Association of the City of Minneapolis in Minnesota," *Korea Daily*, November 14, 1998.

87. Kyung Ok Lee, "About Us," Korean American Women's Association of Minnesota.

88. Dave Alexander, "Advocate Helps Korean Senior Adjust to New Culture," *Star Tribune*, April 6, 1989, 44.

89. Grace Lee, "The History of the Korean Service Center," a congratulatory letter for the fifteenth anniversary, June 2005, Korean Service Center archives.

90. Yunjoo's husband, Pastor Sung Chul Park, is also the founder of the Korean Adoptee Ministry Center. *Korean American Association of Minnesota Newsletter* 1 (2015): 4.

91. Darlene Pfister, "Korean Gardeners Lament Plans to Use Plot for Light-Rail Facility," *Star Tribune*, October 17, 2000, 19; "Garden: It Has Become an Unofficial Cultural Center," *Star Tribune*, September 19, 1991, 4B.

92. "Adopted Korean Children Find Comfort in Discovering, Studying Their Heritage," *Star Tribune*, August 8, 1985, 3; Michelle M. Miller, "'Know Thyself': Adopted Korean Kids Find a Heritage in Camp," *Star Tribune*, August 4, 1988, 1B; Korean Culture Camp of Minnesota, kccmn.org.

93. Korean Heritage House, St. Paul, MN, koreanheritagehouse.com.

94. AK Connection, Minnesota, akconnection.com.

95. Nelson, *Invisible Asians*, 103; Jolene Johnson, "Minneapolis–St. Paul Rising Star Doctors in the Twin Cities," *Mpls. St.Paul Magazine*, April 11, 2018; University of Minnesota Health, "Five Reasons to Consider an Adoption Medicine Clinic Assessment for Your Foster Child."

96. *Minnesota Arirang (Part 2)*.

97. Scott Harron, "Once Upon a Time in Seoul's House of Sweat: An Ambitious American from Duluth Seeks to Hone His Skills in Korea's Demanding Judo College and Gets More Than He Bargained For," *Black Belt* 12, no. 1 (January 1974): 22.

98. Bloomington (MN) Karate Center, bloomingtonkarate.com; Robert Frankovich, *The True Forms of Song Moo Kwan Taekwondo: The Chung Bong Hyung*, Vol. 1 (CreateSpace: Pine Tree Publishing, 2014); Mike Hanks, "Bloomington Karate Center Marks 40 Years," (Bloomington, MN) *Sun Current*, April 11, 2014; Jim Wells, "Tae Kwon Do More Than Karate to Kim," *St. Paul Pioneer Press*, May 20, 1979; *Korean Elderly Society Newsletter*, seventh anniversary edition (1985): 116.

99. Hyun Sook Han, "A Time for a Bigger Community," *Korean American Association of Minnesota Newsletter* 3 (2018): 1.

100. Stephan Huh, "KAAM," *Korean American Association of Minnesota Newsletter* 3 (2015): 5.

101. Han, "A Time for a Bigger Community."

Notes to Sidebars

i. Philip Ahn obituary, *St. Paul Pioneer Press,* November 21, 2006; *Mac Weekly,* April 13, 1956, 1, College Archives Digital Collection, Macalester College.

ii. "Entrepreneur Yun Ho Lee Helped Minnesota's Korean Community, Dies at 91," *St. Paul Pioneer Press,* October 28, 2009; Yun Ho Lee obituary, *St. Paul Pioneer Press,* October 28, 2009; Lee, *My Husband, Yun Ho Lee,* 7–40.

iii. Johng K. Lim, "Lasting Impressions of Mr. Yun Ho Lee," in Lee, *My Husband, Yun Ho Lee,* 107.

iv. Herb Byun, "Elder Lee, A Unique, Fearless Leader," in Lee, *My Husband, Yun Ho Lee,* 121.

v. Chong Hae Jung, "A Man Who Gave," in Lee, *My Husband, Yun Ho Lee,* 87.

vi. *Korean American Association of Minnesota Newsletter* 1 (2014): 5.

vii. Hyun Sook Han, *Many Lives Intertwined* (St. Paul, MN: Yeong & Yeong Book Company, 2004), 191.

viii. Korean American Association of Minnesota, mnkorea.org.

ix. Hannah Yang, "Korean Community Brings Cultural Opportunities for Rochester Children," (Rochester, MN) *Post-Bulletin*, February 9, 2018; Emily Kinzel, "Korea in Eau Claire, Kgam Studio Hopes to Create Art Across Cultures and Help Us Dance Together," *Volume One* (Chippewa Valley, WI), April 5, 2017; Korean Heritage House.

x. Misuk Palmer (former MAKA president), "To the pastors of all Minnesota Korean churches," letter to the Minnesota Korean Church Association, March 9, 2018.

xi. Crystal Lee Hyun Joo Chappell, "Korean-American Adoptees Organize for Support," *Star Tribune,* December 29, 1996, E7.

xii. Susan March, "Deep Connections for Minnesota's Adopted Koreans," *Twin Cities Daily Planet,* December 22, 2010; Korean Adoptees Ministry Center, Roseville, MN.

xiii. *Korean Quarterly*.

xiv. "We Wanted to Deliver the Sound of Excitement Shinparam to the United States," *Hankook Iblo,* October 14, 2013, 28; Shinparam Facebook page.

xv. Susie Voss, "Minnesota's First Korean Immersion School May Benefit Adoptees," *Twin Cities Daily Planet,* August 27, 2015; Tesha M. Christensen, "Korean Immersion School Opens in St. Paul," *St. Paul Monitor,* December 10, 2014; "The First Korean Dual Language School Opens in Minnesota," *Yon Hap News,* October 8, 2014; Sejong Academy, St. Paul, MN.

Index

Italicized page numbers indicate photos, illustrations, diagrams, or captions.

Picture Credits

page 4: American National Red Cross photograph collection, Library of Congress, 1919–1929, anrc 14947

page 6: "A War Bride Named 'Blue' Comes Home," *LIFE* magazine 31, no. 19 (November 1951): 41

page 14: US Census Bureau, 2011–16 American Community Survey. Map created by Zain Kaiser.

pages 15, 17 top and bottom, 18, 29, 30, 49, 50, 57, 65, 66: Minnesota Historical Society photo collections

pages 20, 51, 53, 60, 63, 90: Soon Ja Lee

page 21: Neal L. Gault Jr. Papers, N. S. Gault papers, Photographs, 1940–2005 folder, box 2, collection 1168, University of Minnesota archives

page 22: Macy Harold papers, Korea photographs folder, box 2, collection 273, University of Minnesota archives

pages 33, 35, 42, 43, 56, 74: Courtesy author

pages 36, 79, 82: Stephen Wunrow

page 39: Created by Siyong Park

pages 41, 83: Insun Hong

page 45: Brooke Newmaster

page 54: Created by Zain Kaiser

page 61: Korean American Association of Minnesota archives

pages 70, 86: Mehee Coolidge

page 71: Stephen Wunrow, *Korean Quarterly*

page 72: Korean Service Center

page 77: Photo by Jeff Wheeler, Minneapolis Star Tribune Portraits: An Inventory of Its Portrait Collection, 1901–1988, folder Korean community 1980–1988, box 151, Minnesota Historical Society

page 78: Sung Chul Park

page 81: *Korean Quarterly*

page 84: Sejong Academy

Acknowledgments

I am honored to have had the chance to document the story of Koreans in Minnesota. This book would not have been completed without help from members of Minnesota's Korean community. My deepest thanks go to all I've met and interviewed during the research process, including Chang Won Song, Hyun Sook Han, Tae Hwan Kim, Yunjoo Park, Sung Chul Park, Ji Suk Jung, Soon Ja Lee, Changjae Lee, Insun Hong, Stephan Huh, John Choi, Hak Cheol Shin, Brooke Newmaster, Stephen Wunrow and Martha Vickery, Chil Yong Kwon, Noyeul Priestess, Nicole Johnson, Yeon Joo Cho, Kyeonghe Kim, and Changseung Yoo. All have been extremely helpful in sharing their own stories and/or connecting me with others who contributed to the research.

I am especially thankful to Shannon Pennefeather for her excellent editing but most of all for always being so positive and enthusiastic throughout the entire process.

For moral and financial support, I owe special thanks to the members of the political science department of the University of Wisconsin–River Falls—Neil Kraus, Davida Alperin, and Wes Chapin—and to John Heppen in Geography. I also thank Michelle Parkinson for her work in revising and editing the early draft. Special recognition is owed to Betty Bergland, who freely shared her expert advice and helped me navigate the archives, teaching me the joy and hardship of working with primary sources.

I am grateful to my family in Korea, especially my father, Jih-Hoon Ryu, for being a wonderful listener and teacher, and my father-in-law, Han Soo Cha, for his emotional support.

Finally, my utmost love and gratitude belong to my husband, Dongwuk Cha, for his unconditional and unwavering support, and to my three boys, Patrick, Aiden, and Declan, for being so patient and understanding.

Minnesotans can trace their families and their state's heritage to a multitude of ethnic groups. *The People of Minnesota* series tells each group's story in a compact, handsomely illustrated, and accessible paperback. Readers will learn about the group's accomplishments, ethnic organizations, settlement patterns, and occupations. Each book includes a personal story of one person or family, told through a diary, a letter, or an oral history.

Minnesota writer Bill Holm reminded us why these stories remain as important as ever: "To be ethnic, somehow, is to be human. Neither can we escape it, nor should we want to. You cannot interest yourself in the lives of your neighbors if you don't take sufficient interest in your own."

This series is based on the critically acclaimed book *They Chose Minnesota: A Survey of the State's Ethnic Groups* (Minnesota Historical Society Press). The volumes in *The People of Minnesota* bring each group's story up to date and add dozens of photographs to inform and enhance the telling.

Books in the series include *Swedes in Minnesota, Jews in Minnesota, Norwegians in Minnesota, African Americans in Minnesota,* and *Germans in Minnesota.*

About the Author

Sooh-Rhee Ryu is an associate professor of political science at the University of Wisconsin–River Falls. Her research and teaching focus on South Korean politics, Asian American politics, international relations, and the politics of developing countries.